KV-514-796

The Diamond as Big as the Ritz and Other Stories

F. Scott Fitzgerald

Hong Kong
OXFORD UNIVERSITY PRESS
Oxford Singapore Tokyo

Oxford University Press

Oxford London New York Toronto
Kuala Lumpur Singapore Hong Kong Tokyo
Delhi Bombay Calcutta Madras Karachi
Nairobi Dar es Salaam Cape Town
Melbourne Auckland

and associated companies in
Beirut Berlin Ibadan Mexico City Nicosia

OXFORD is a trade mark of Oxford University Press

The stories in this volume are adapted and abridged with the permission of The Bodley Head from the The Bodley Head Scott Fitzgerald as follows: The Diamond as Big as the Ritz, The Bodley Head Scott Fitzgerald Volume 5; Basil: The Freshest Boy and Babylon Revisited, The Bodley Head Scott Fitzgerald Volume 6; Gretchen's Forty Winks, The Bodley Head Scott Fitzgerald Volume 3 (1st edition)

Retold by Benjamin Chia
Illustrated by Kathryn Blomfield
Simplified according to the language grading scheme
especially compiled by D. H. Howe

ISBN 0 19 581364 2

Printed in Hong Kong by Ko's Arts Printing Co.
Published by Oxford University Press, Warwick House, Hong Kong

Oxford Progressive English Readers
General Editor: D.H. Howe

The Diamond As Big As the Ritz
and Other Stories

The *Oxford Progressive English Readers* series provides a wide range of reading for learners of English. It includes classics, the favourite stories of young readers, and also modern fiction. The series has five grades: the *Introductory Grade* at a 1400 word level, *Grade 1* at a 2100 word level, *Grade 2* at a 3100 word level, *Grade 3* at a 3700 word level and *Grade 4* which consists of abridged stories. Structural as well as lexical controls are applied at each level.

Wherever possible the mood and style of the original stories have been retained. Where this requires departure from the grading scheme, glosses and notes are given.

All the books in the series are attractively illustrated. Each book also has a short section containing questions and suggested activities for students.

Contents

F. Scott Fitzgerald was born in 1894 in the USA. He was educated at the University of Princeton then served as an officer in the armed forces during World War I.

His works, which caught the flavour and interests of the changing era, include both full length novels and short stories. *The Diamond as Big as the Ritz* is probably one of his best-known short stories. It considers, with irony and pathos, contemporary life related to the "American Dream".

F. Scott Fitzgerald has become one of America's most famous writers of fiction. He died in 1940.

1

The Diamond As Big As The Ritz

JOHN T. UNGER came from a family that had been well-known in Hades* — a small town on the Mississippi River — for several generations. John's parents were known for taking an active part in golf and politics. Young John T. Unger, who had just turned sixteen, always kept up with the fashion of   5
the day. And now, for a certain time, he was to be away from home. His parents thought it best that he should go to St Midas's School near Boston — Hades was too small to hold their darling and gifted son.

Before he left, his mother packed his trunks full of things   10
she thought he might need, and his father gave him a wallet filled with money.

'Remember, you are always welcome here,' he said. 'You can be sure, boy, that we'll keep the home fires burning.'

'I know,' answered John huskily.   15

'Don't forget who you are and where you come from,' continued his father proudly, 'and you will do nothing to harm yourself. You are an Unger — from Hades.'

So the old man and the young man shook hands and John walked away with tears streaming from his eyes. Outside the   20
city, he stopped to glance back for the last time. The lights of Hades against the sky seemed so warm and beautiful.

St Midas's School is half an hour from Boston by car. It is the most expensive and the most exclusive boys' school in the world.   25

John's first two years there passed pleasantly. The fathers of all the boys were money-kings and John spent his summers visiting fashionable resorts*. While he was very fond of all the boys he visited, their fathers seemed to him to be much the

---

Hades, the name of the town where John lived but also the equivalent of Hell in Greek Mythology. *resorts*, places where people spend their holidays.

same. Whenever he told them where his home was, they all made the same joke, asking, 'Pretty hot down there?' or 'Is it hot enough for you down there?' which he hated.

5 In the middle of his second year at school, a quiet, handsome boy named Percy Washington had been put in John's form. The newcomer was pleasant in his manner and very well dressed even for St Midas's, but for some reason he stayed away from the other boys. The only person with whom he was friendly was John T. Unger. But even to John
10 he never talked about his home or his family. That he was wealthy went without saying. When Percy invited him to spend the summer at his home, he accepted at once.

It was only when they were in the train that Percy talked about his family.

15 'My father,' he said, 'is by far the richest man in the world.'

'Oh,' said John, politely. He could think of no other answer.

'By far the richest,' repeated Percy.

'I was reading,' began John, 'that there was one man in America with an income of over five million a year and
20 four men with incomes of over three million a year, and —'

'Oh, they're nothing. My father could buy them out and not know he'd done it.'

'He must be very rich,' said John simply. 'I'm glad. I like very rich people. I visited the Schulitzer-Murphys last Easter.
25 Vivian Schulitzer-Murphy had rubies* as big as hens' eggs, and —'

'I love jewels,' agreed Percy enthusiastically, 'of course I wouldn't want anyone at school to know about it, but I've got quite a collection myself. I used to collect them
30 instead of stamps.'

'And diamonds,' continued John eagerly. 'The Schulitzer-Murphys had diamonds as big as walnuts —'

'That's nothing.' Percy had leaned forward and dropped his voice to a low whisper. 'That's nothing at all. My father
35 has a diamond bigger than the Ritz-Carlton Hotel*.'

*rubies, precious stones, red in colour. *the Ritz-Carlton Hotel, a famous New York hotel.

They arrive

In the evening the train stopped at a small village some-where in Montana. A small horse-drawn carriage, which seemed to appear from nowhere, came and drove them away.

After half an hour, the evening sky had grown dark. *5* The driver called out to an object standing in the dim light ahead of them. In answer to his call, it turned a bright light on them which looked at them like an unfriendly eye. As they came closer, John saw that it was the tail-light of an immense car, large and more magnificent than *10* any he had ever seen.

'Get in,' said Percy to his friend. 'Sorry we had to bring you this far in that buggy, but of course we can't let the people on the train and from the village see this.'

'What a car!' cried John, in amazement. *15*

'This thing?' Percy laughed. 'Why, it's just an old worthless thing.'

By this time they were driving along through the darkness towards the break between the two mountains.

'We'll be there in an hour and a half,' said Percy, looking *20* at the clock. 'I may as well tell you it's not going to be like anything you ever saw before.'

They had now reached and were entering the break between the two mountains and almost immediately the way became much rougher. *25*

'Rocky, you see. An ordinary car would be knocked to pieces in half an hour. You notice we're going uphill now.'

In a few minutes the car was crossing a high rise, where they caught a glimpse of a pale moon which had just risen in the distance. The car stopped suddenly and some men *30* appeared from the dark. They set to work and four immense cables came down from above and were tied to the wheels of the car. John felt the car being lifted slowly from the ground, up and up, then higher, until he could see the valley that they had just left. Only on one side there was still rock, and then *35*

3

suddenly there was no rock beside them or anywhere around.

In a moment they were down again, and finally they landed on the smooth earth.

'The worst is over,' said Percy looking out of the window.
5 'It's only five miles from here, and our own road all the way. This belongs to us. This is where the United States ends, father says.'

'Are we in Canada?'

'We are not. We're in the middle of the Montana Rockies.
10 But you are now on the only five square miles of land in the country that's never been put on a map.'

'Why hasn't it? Did they forget it?'

'No,' said Percy, 'they tried to do it three times. The first time my grandfather corrupted a whole department,
15 the second time he had the official maps of the United States worked on. That held them for fifteen years. The last time was harder. My father fixed it so that their compass did not work. They thought it was a town ten miles farther up the valley. There's only one thing my father's
20 afraid of,' he concluded, 'only one thing in the world that could be used to find us out.'

'What's that?'

Percy sank his voice to a whisper.

'Aeroplanes,' he breathed. 'We've got half-a-dozen anti-
25 aircraft guns and we've arranged it so far — but there have been a few deaths and we've taken a great many prisoners. Not that we mind that, father and I, but it upsets mother and the girls and there's always the chance that some time we won't be able to arrange it.'

30 Outside the Montana night was as bright as day. The brick road was smooth as they drove around a still, moonlit lake; they passed into darkness for a moment, then they came out onto a broad lawn.

In the light of the stars John could see a castle of bright
35 shining marble on the edge of a lake. The many towers, the wonder of a thousand yellow windows with their many different shapes of golden light, the star-shine and blue

4

shade, all played on John's spirit like music. An arrangement of lights at the top of one of the tallest towers made it like a sort of floating fairyland. As John gazed up in wonder the faint sound of violins playing drifted down like nothing he had ever heard before. Then in a moment the car stopped 5 before wide, high marble steps. The night air was filled with the scent of flowers. At the top of the steps two great doors swung open silently and a beautiful lady with black hair held out her arms towards them.

'Mother,' Percy was saying, 'this is my friend, John Unger, 10 from Hades.'

Afterwards John remembered that first night as a rainbow-coloured dream of music soft as a voice in love, and of the beauty of things, lights and shadows, and motions and faces. There was a white-haired man who stood drinking 15 from a gold cup. There was a girl with a face like a flower, and precious blue stones in her hair. There were rooms with walls of gold, ceilings lined with diamonds of every size and shape, crystal lamps of all colours, and furs of every sort. Between them were corridors of the palest ivory. 20 And then they were at dinner. The surrounding riches and luxury seemed to overpower him. He tried sleepily to answer a question put to him.

'Yes,' he replied with a polite effort, 'it certainly is hot enough for me down there.' 25

He managed to add a ghostly laugh; then, without move-ment, he seemed to float off and away . . . He fell asleep.

When he awoke he knew that several hours had passed. He was in a great quiet room. His young host was standing over him. 30

'You fell asleep at dinner,' Percy was saying. 'I nearly did, too — it was so good to be comfortable again after this year of school. Servants undressed and bathed you while you were sleeping.'

'Is this a bed or a cloud?' sighed John. 'Percy, Percy — 35 before you go, I want to apologize.'

'For what?'

5

'For doubting you when you said you had a diamond as big as the Ritz-Carlton Hotel.'

Percy smiled.

'I thought you didn't believe me. It's that mountain, you know.'

'What mountain?'

'The mountain the castle rests on. It's not very big for a mountain. Except for about fifty feet of earth and stone on top it's solid diamond. One diamond, one cubic mile without a flaw. Aren't you listening? Say —'

But John T. Unger had fallen asleep again.

The next day

Morning. As he awoke he felt that the room had at the same moment become dense with sunlight. One part of the wall opened up to the day. A servant in a white uniform stood beside his bed.

'Good evening,' said John, trying to remember where he was.

'Good morning, sir. Are you ready for your bath, sir? Oh, don't get up — I'll put you in — there. Thank you, sir.'

John lay quietly as his pyjamas were removed — he was amused and delighted; he expected to be lifted like a child but nothing of the sort happened; instead he felt the bed rise up slowly on its side — he began to roll in the direction of the wall, but when he reached the wall its drapery gave way, and he was put gently into water the same temperature as his body.

He had been brought into another chamber and was sitting in a sunken bath with his head just above the level of the floor. All around him, and the bottom of the bath itself, was a blue aquarium*, and gazing through the crystal surface on which he sat, he could see fish swimming. From overhead, sunlight came down through sea-green glass.

*aquarium, a fish tank.

'I suppose, sir, that you'd like hot rosewater this morning, sir — and perhaps cold salt water to finish.'

The servant was standing beside him.

'Yes,' agreed John, smiling in a silly way, 'as you please.'
5 This was quite beyond his experience — ordering his bath.

'Shall I turn on the moving-picture machine, sir?' suggested the servant. 'There's a good comedy in this machine today, or I can put in a serious piece in a moment, if you prefer.'

'No, thanks,' answered John, politely but firmly. He
10 was enjoying his bath too much to want to do anything else. In a moment he was listening to the sound of music from just outside, music that was in keeping with the fall of the bath water.

When he finished his bath, he was rubbed with oil, alcohol,
15 and spice. Afterwards, he was shaved and his hair was trimmed in the greatest comfort.

'Mr Percy is waiting in your sitting-room,' said the servant, when all was done. 'My name is Gygsum, Mr Unger, sir. I am to see to Mr Unger every morning.'

20 John walked out into the sunshine of his living-room, where he found breakfast waiting for him. Percy was also there, smoking in an easy chair.

Percy tells the story

This is a story of the Washington family as Percy outlined it for John during breakfast.

25 The father of the present Mr Washington had been a direct descendant of George Washington, and Lord Baltimore. At the close of the Civil War he was a twenty-five-year-old Colonel left with about a thousand dollars in gold.

The young Colonel decided to go West to try his luck.
30 When he had been in Montana for less than a month and things were going very poorly indeed, he came upon his great discovery. He had lost his way when riding in the hills, and after a day without food he began to grow hungry.

As he was without his gun, he was forced to chase a squirrel. While he was at it, he saw something shiny in the squirrel's mouth. Just before it disappeared into its hole it dropped its burden. It was a large and perfect diamond.

Late that night he found his way to camp and brought 5 all his slaves with him to dig for more diamonds. To his utter amazement, the mountain was diamond — it was nothing else but solid diamond. He filled four bags full of glittering samples and rode back to town. There he managed to sell half a dozen small stones — when he tried 10 a larger one a storekeeper fainted and he was arrested as a public disturber. He escaped from jail and caught the train for New York, where he sold a few medium-sized diamonds and received about two hundred thousand dollars in gold. But he did not dare sell more — in fact, he left 15 New York just in time. People began to talk about a diamond mine being discovered. It started a diamond rush. But by that time he was on his way back to Montana.

In two weeks he had calculated that the diamond in the mountain was almost equal in quantity to all the rest of 20 the diamonds known to exist in the world. It was not possible to find out its exact worth. If it was offered for sale, there would not be enough gold in the world to buy a tenth part of it. And what could anyone do with a diamond that size? 25

It was an amazing situation. He was, in one sense, the richest man that ever lived — and yet was he worth anything at all? Diamond discovered in such a large quantity could spoil the market. If the government found out about it, they might take it over from him to protect the market. 30 There was nothing he could do but sell his discovery in secret.

He went abroad. He sailed to Russia and India with one hundred thousand dollars and two trunks filled with rough diamonds of all sizes. Six months after his departure from 35 Montana he was in St Petersburg. He took obscure lodgings and called immediately upon the court jeweller, announcing

9

that he had a diamond for the Czar. He remained in St Petersburg for two weeks, in constant danger of being murdered, living from lodging to lodging, and afraid of visiting his trunks more than three or four times during
5   the whole fortnight.

On his promise to return in a year with larger and finer stones, he was allowed to leave for India. After he left, he visited the capitals of twenty-two countries and talked with five emperors, eleven kings and three princes. At that
10   time, he calculated his own wealth at one billion dollars.

From 1870 until his death in 1900, the history of Fitz-Norman Washington was a long story in gold. He married, brought up a single son, murdered his own brother because he had got into the habit of drinking and nearly told others
15   their secret. Very few other murders affected these happy years of progress.

Just before he died, he turned his wealth into gold and put it in banks all over the world. His son followed this policy and went a step further. He changed his gold into
20   the rarest of all elements — radium — so that a billion dollars in gold could be put into something no bigger than a cigar box.

When Fitz-Norman had been dead for three years, his son decided that the business had gone far enough. The amount
25   of wealth that he and his father had taken out of the mountain was beyond exact calculation. Then he did a very simple thing — he sealed up the mine. What had been taken out of it would support all the Washingtons for generations. His one care must be the protection of his secret.
30   This was the family among whom John T. Unger was staying. This was the story he heard in his silver-walled living-room the morning after his arrival.

John meets Kismine

After breakfast, John found his way out through the great

marble entrance, and set off along a walk of white and blue brick that seemed to lead in no particular direction.

John turned a corner. Then he saw a girl coming towards him over the grass. She was the most beautiful person he had ever seen. 5

She was dressed in a little white dress that came just below her knees. Her pink bare feet scattered the dew before them as she came. She was younger than John — not more than sixteen.

'Hello,' she cried softly, 'I'm Kismine.' 10

She was much more than that to John already.

'You haven't met me,' said her soft voice. 'You met my sister, Jasmine, last night. I was not feeling well.'

'How do you do?' he said. 'I hope you're better this morning.' 15

John noticed that they had been walking along the path. On her suggestion they sat down together.

He was critical* about women. A single defect — a thick ankle, a coarse voice, a glass eye — was enough to make him lose interest. Here for the first time in his life he was 20 beside a girl who seemed to him perfection.

'Are you from the East?' asked Kismine with interest.

'No,' answered John simply. 'I'm from Hades.'

'I'm going East to school this fall,' she said. 'D'you think I'll like it? I'm going to New York to Miss Bulge's. It's 25 very strict.'

'Your father wants you to be proud,' observed John.

'We are,' she answered, her eyes shining with dignity. 'None of us has ever been punished. Father said we never should be. Once when my sister Jasmine was a little girl 30 she pushed him downstairs and he just got up and limped away.'

'Mother was — well, a little shocked,' continued Kismine, 'when she heard that you were from — from where you are from, you know. But then, you see, she's a Spaniard 35 and old-fashioned.'

*critical, fault-finding.

I I

'Do you spend much time out here?' asked John, to hide the fact that he was somewhat hurt by this remark.

'Percy and Jasmine and I are here every summer. I'm very innocent and girlish. I never smoke, or drink, or read anything except poetry. I know hardly any mathematics or chemistry. I dress very simply — in fact, I scarcely dress at all. I believe that girls ought to enjoy their youth in a wholesome way.'

'I do too,' said John heartily.

'I like you,' she whispered. 'Are you going to spend all your time with Percy while you're here, or will you be nice to me? I've never had a boy in love with me in all my life. I've never been allowed even to see boys alone — except Percy. I came all the way out here hoping to run into you, where the family wouldn't be around.'

Deeply flattered, John bowed as he had been taught at dancing school in Hades.

'We'd better go now,' said Kismine sweetly. 'I have to be with mother at eleven. You haven't asked me to kiss you once. I thought boys always did that nowadays.'

John drew himself up proudly.

'Some of them do,' he answered, 'but not me. Girls don't do that sort of thing — in Hades.'

Side by side they walked back towards the house.

John stood facing Mr Braddock Washington in the full sunlight. The elder man was about forty with a proud face, intelligent eyes, and a strong healthy figure. He carried a plain walking-stick with a single large precious stone. He and Percy were showing John around.

'The slaves' quarters are there.' His walking-stick pointed to a row of marble houses. There are about two hundred and fifty now. You notice that they've lived so long apart from the world that they seem to speak a different language.

'This is the golf-course,' he continued, as they strolled along the smooth winter grass.

He smiled pleasantly at John.

'Many men in the cage, father?' asked Percy suddenly.

'One less than there should be,' he said angrily — and then added after a moment, 'We've had difficulties.'

'Mother was telling me,' said Percy, 'that Italian teacher —'

'A terrible mistake,' said Braddock Washington. 'But
5 of course there's a good chance that we may have got him. Perhaps he fell somewhere in the woods or over a cliff. And then probably if he did get away his story wouldn't be believed. Nevertheless, I've had two dozen men looking for him in different towns around here.'

10 'And no luck?'

'Some. Fourteen of them reported that they'd each killed a man answering to that description, but of course it was probably only the reward they were after —'

He broke off. They had come to a large hole in the ground
15 covered by strong iron bars. Braddock Washington pointed his cane at the hole. John stepped to the edge and gazed. Immediately he heard shouting from below.

'Come on down to Hell!'

'Hello, my boy, how's the air up there?'

20 'Hey! Throw us a rope!'

It was too dark to see clearly into the hole below. Then Mr Washington put out his cane and touched a button in the grass, and the scene below lit up.

'These are some adventurers who had the misfortune
25 to discover the Mountain,' he remarked.

Below them there had appeared a large hollow in the earth shaped like the inside of a bowl. The sides were steep and of polished glass and on its bottom stood about two dozen men in aviators'* uniforms. They seemed to be a
30 well-fed, healthy lot.

Braddock Washington drew a garden chair to the edge of the hollow and sat down.

'Well, how are you, boys?' he asked in a friendly tone.

A tall man moved apart from the others, and held up his
35 hand.

'Let me ask you a few questions!' he cried. 'You pretend

aviators, people who fly aeroplanes.

to be a fair-minded man.'

'How could a man of my position be fair-minded towards you? You might as well speak of being fair-minded towards a piece of steak.'

'All right!' he cried. 'We've argued this out before. How about trusting us to keep your secret?'

'You don't make that suggestion seriously,' said Washington. 'I did take out one man to teach my daughter Italian. Last week he got away.'

This caused the prisoners suddenly to cheer and dance and sing with joy.

Braddock Washington sat in silence until they were quiet again.

'You see,' he continued, 'I bear you no ill-will. I like to see you enjoying yourselves. That's why I didn't tell you the whole story at once. The man — what was his name? — was shot by some of my agents in fourteen different places.'

Not guessing that the places referred to were cities, the rejoicing stopped immediately.

Mr Washington reached forward suddenly with his cane and pushed the button in the grass. The picture below went out instantly, and there remained only darkness and silence again.

Mr Washington, followed by the two boys, walked slowly towards the meadow which was bright with flowers.

In love

July on the diamond mountain was a month of soft nights and of warm, glowing days. John and Kismine were in love.

Late one afternoon when the music room was quiet, they spent an hour there together. He held her hand and she gave him such a look that he whispered her name. She bent towards him — then hesitated.

'Did you say "Kismine"?' she asked softly, 'or — '

She had wanted to be sure. She thought she might have misunderstood.

Neither of them had ever kissed before, but in the course of an hour it seemed to make little difference.

5   The afternoon drifted away. They had decided to be married as soon as possible.

They decide to elope

Every day Mr Washington and the two young men went hunting or fishing in the deep forests or played golf or swam in the mountain coolness of the lake. John found
10   Mr Washington utterly disinterested in any ideas or opinions except his own. Mrs Washington kept her distance at all times. She paid little attention to her two daughters, and was entirely absorbed in her son Percy, with whom she held endless conversations in rapid Spanish at dinner.

15   Jasmine the elder daughter looked like Kismine but was not quite as attractive. Her favourite books were about girls in poor families.

John was enchanted by the wonders of the castle and the valley.

20   Talking to Percy, he asked, 'Who designed your wonderful house?'

'Well,' answered Percy, 'I blush to tell you, but it was a moving-picture fellow. He was the only man we found who was used to playing with an unlimited amount of
25   money, though he couldn't read or write.'

As August drew to a close John began to regret that he must soon go back to school. He and Kismine had decided to elope the following June.

'It would be nicer to be married here,' Kismine confessed,
30   'but of course I could never get father's permission to marry you at all. Next to that I'd rather elope.'

One afternoon late in August something that Kismine

said changed the face of the entire situation, and terrified John.

They were in their favourite corner and between kisses he said sadly, 'Sometimes I think we'll never marry, you're too wealthy. No one as rich as you are can be like other 5 girls. I should marry the daughter of some well-to-do businessman and be content with her half-million.'

'I knew someone like that once,' remarked Kismine. 'I don't think you'd have been happy with her. She was a friend of my sister's. She visited here.' 10

'Oh, then you've had other guests?' John said in surprise.

Kismine seemed to regret her words.

'Oh, yes,' she said hurriedly, 'we've had a few.'

'But aren't you — wasn't your father afraid they'd talk outside?' 15

'Oh, to some extent, to some extent,' she answered. 'Let's talk about something more pleasant.'

But John's curiosity was aroused.

'Something more pleasant!' he demanded. 'What's unpleasant about that? Weren't they nice girls?' 20

To his great surprise Kismine began to weep.

'Yes — th — that's the — the whole t-trouble. I grew qu-quite attached to some of them. So did Jasmine, but she kept inv-viting them anyway. I couldn't understand it.'

A dark suspicion was born in John's heart. 25

'Do you mean that they told, and your father had them — removed?'

'Worse than that,' she said brokenly. 'Father took no chances — and Jasmine kept writing, asking them to come, and they had such a good time!' 30

She was overcome with grief.

Horrified by what he had heard, John sat there open-mouthed.

'Now, I've told you, and I shouldn't have,' she said, calming suddenly and drying her dark blue eyes. 35

'Do you mean to say that your father had them murdered before they left?'

She nodded.

'In August usually — or early in September. It's only natural for us to get all the pleasure out of them that we can first.'

5   'How terrible! How — why, I must be going crazy! Did you really admit that — '

'I did,' interrupted Kismine, shrugging her shoulders. 'We can't very well imprison them like those aviators, where they'd be a continual reproach to us every day. And it's
10 always been made easier for Jasmine and me, because father had it done sooner than we expected. In that way we avoided any farewell scenes — '

'So you murdered them! Uh!' cried John.

'It was done very nicely. They were drugged while they
15 were asleep — and their families were always told that they died of some disease.'

'But — I fail to understand why you kept on inviting them!'

'I didn't,' burst out Kismine. 'I never invited one. Jasmine
20 did. And they always had a very good time. She'd give them the nicest presents towards the end. I shall probably have visitors too — I'll not feel so terrible about it. We can't let such an inevitable* thing as death stand in the way of enjoying life while we have it. Think how lonesome
25 it'd be out here if we never had any one. Why, father and mother have sacrificed some of their best friends just as we have.'

'And so,' cried John, 'and so you were letting me make love to you and pretending to return it, and talking about
30 marriage, all the time knowing perfectly well that I'd never get out of here alive — '

'No,' she protested. 'Not any more. I did at first. You were here. I couldn't help that, and I thought your last days might as well be pleasant for both of us. But then
35 I fell in love with you, and — and I'm honestly sorry you're going to be put away — though I'd rather you'd be put

*inevitable, unable to avoid.

away than ever kiss another girl.'

'Oh, you would, would you?' cried John fiercely.

'Much rather. Besides, I've always heard that a girl can have more fun with a man whom she knows she can never marry. Oh, why did I tell you? I've probably spoiled your whole good time now, and we were really enjoying things when you didn't know. I knew it would make things unpleasant for you.'

'Oh you did, did you?' John's voice trembled with anger. 'I've heard just about enough of this. If you think it amusing to have an affair with a fellow that you know isn't much better than a corpse, I don't want to have anymore to do with you!'

'You're not a corpse!' she protested in horror. 'You're not a corpse! I won't have you saying that I kissed a corpse!'

'I said nothing of the sort!'

'You did! You said I kissed a corpse!'

'I didn't!'

Their voices had risen, but upon hearing footsteps coming in their direction, they both became silent. A moment later, they found Braddock Washington staring at them through the rose bushes.

'What are you two doing here, anyhow?' he demanded harshly. 'Kismine, you ought to be — to be reading or playing golf with your sister. Go read! Go play golf! Don't let me find you here when I come back!'

Then he bowed at John and went up the path.

'See?' said Kismine angrily, when he was out of hearing. 'you've spoiled it all. We can never meet any more. He won't let me meet you. He'd have you poisoned if he thought we were in love.'

'We're not, any more!' cried John, 'so he doesn't have to worry about it. Moreover, don't fool yourself that I'm going to stay around here. In six hours I'll be over those mountains, no matter what I'll have to do.'

They had both got to their feet, and at this remark Kismine came close and put her arm through his.

'I'm going, too.'

'You must be crazy — '

'Of course I'm going,' she interrupted patiently.

His love for her returned. She was his — she would go
5 with him to share his dangers. After all she loved him; she
had saved him, in fact.

Discussing the matter, they decided that since Braddock
Washington had seen them together they would depart
the next night.

The battle

10 Long after midnight John was woken suddenly from
his uneasy dreams. He sat up in bed and heard a sharp noise
just outside his room. Then someone appeared at the door.
He felt his life was in danger.

With a sudden movement of fright John pressed the
15 button by his bedside. The next moment he was sitting
in the green sunken bath of the adjoining room.

He sprang out wet and cold, and ran for the door. The
next thing he knew he found himself standing on the ivory
landing of the grand staircase which led down to the hall.
20 There was a single lamp burning in the great round ceiling.
For a moment John hesitated, overcome by the silent
splendour that surrounded him.

Then two things happened at once. Three naked Negroes
came into the hall and Braddock Washington appeared in
25 the lift. It came into John's mind at once that they might
be the men sent to kill him.

'Get in here! All three of you! Quick as hell!' Braddock
Washington shouted.

Immediately the three Negroes ran into the lift, something
30 terribly serious had happened, something more urgent
than his murder. John did not know. He heard the lift go up
and down. It was probable that Percy was hurrying to help
his father. It occurred to John that this was his opportunity

to join Kismine and plan an immediate escape. He waited until the lift had been silent for several minutes. Then he returned to his room and dressed quickly.

When he reached Kismine's suite, the door of her sitting-room was open and the lamps were lighted. Kismine stood   5
near the window of the room listening and as John entered noiselessly, she turned towards him.

'Oh, it's you!' she whispered, crossing the room to him. 'Did you hear them?'

'I heard your father's slaves in my — '   10

'No,' she interrupted excitedly. 'Aeroplanes!'

'Aeroplanes? Perhaps that was the sound that woke me.'

'There're at least a dozen. I saw one a few moments ago against the moon. The guard back by the cliff fired his rifle and that's what woke father up. We're going to open   15
fire on them right away.'

'Are they here on purpose?'

'Yes — it's that Italian who got away — '

'Come on!' he cried to him. 'We'll go up to the roof garden, and watch from there!'   20

Above, under the moon, flew a dozen bombers in a circle. From here and there in the valleys guns were fired at them. Kismine clapped her hands with pleasure, which a moment later turned to dismay as the aeroplanes began to drop their bombs and the valley went up in flames.   25

After that the aeroplanes concentrated their attack on the gun points on the ground. Soon one of them was knocked out.

The aim of the aeroplanes was becoming more and more precise and only two guns were left to fire back. It was   30
obvious that they could not hold out much longer.

'Come on!' cried John, pulling Kismine's arm, 'we've got to go. Do you realize that those aviators will kill you without question if they find you?'

She left the roof garden unwillingly.   35

'We'll have to wake Jasmine!' she said, as they hurried towards the lift. Then she added with a sort of childish delight, 'We'll be poor, won't we? Like people in books. And I'll be an orphan and utterly free. Free and poor! What fun!' She stopped and raised her lips to him in a delighted kiss.

'It's impossible to be both together,' said John grimly.
5 'People have found that out. And I should choose to be free rather than poor. As an extra caution you'd better take your jewellery with you.'

Ten minutes later the two girls met John in the dark corridor. Passing for the last time through the splendid halls,
10 they stood for a moment out on the terrace, watching the battle. There now remained only one gun in action.

Kismine led them to a hidden spot from where they could watch the wild night in the valley and escape when it should be necessary.

Escape!

15 It was three o'clock when they reached their destination. Jasmine fell off to sleep immediately, leaning against the trunk of a large tree. John and Kismine sat, his arm around her, and watched the dying battle. Shortly after four o'clock the last gun went out of action in a tongue of red smoke.
20 The aeroplanes were circling and getting closer to the ground. When they made certain there was no more armed resistance, they would land, and that would be the end of the Washingtons.

As the firing stopped, the valley grew quiet. The castle
25 stood dark and silent, beautiful without light as it had been beautiful in the sun. Then John noticed that Kismine, like her sister, had fallen sound asleep.

It was long after four when he became aware of foot steps along the path they had followed. John held his breath
30 and waited until the steps had gone a safe distance up the mountain. Then he followed. Coming to a high boulder, he lifted his head gradually above its edge. He saw Braddock Washington standing there on the top of the mountain

against the grey sky without sound or sign of life. Dawn was breaking and the sky was slowly turning light. For a moment, he remained there absorbed in some deep thoughts. Then he signalled to the two Negroes at his feet to lift the burden which lay between them. As they struggled upright, 5 the first rays of the sun struck through an immense and beautifully cut diamond. It shone like a morning star.

After a while the white man lifted his head and slowly raised his arms in a gesture of attention, as one who would call a great crowd to listen. But there was no crowd, only 10 the silence of the mountain and the sky, broken by birds down among the trees. He began to speak in a voice that still showed great pride.

'You out there — ,' he cried in a trembling voice. 'You — there — !' He paused, his arms still raised, his head held 15 attentively as though he were waiting for an answer. John looked around to see whether there might be men coming down the mountain, but the mountain was bare. There was only sky and wind in the tree-tops. Could Washington be praying? For a moment John wondered. 20

'Oh, you above there!'

The voice was strong and confident. It was not how one would plead.

'You there — '

Words, too quickly said to be understood, were flowing 25 one into the other . . . John listened breathlessly, catching a phrase here and there, while the voice broke off, went on, broke off again. Suddenly he realised that Braddock Washington was offering a bribe to God!

That was it — there was no doubt. The diamond in the 30 arms of his slaves was some advance sample, a promise of more to follow.

He would give to God, he continued, as an offering, the greatest diamond in the world. This diamond would be cut and shaped to perfection. Many men would work upon it for 35 many years. It would be set in a great dome of beaten gold, wonderfully carved and equipped with gates of opal and sapphire. In the middle would be a chapel presided over by an altar of iridescent*, everchanging radium which would burn out the eyes of any worshipper who lifted up his head from prayer.

5   In return he asked only a simple thing, a thing that for God would be very easy — only that matters should be as they were yesterday at this hour and that they should so remain. So very simple! Let the heavens open swallowing these men and their aeroplanes — and then close again.
10 Let him have his slaves once more, restored to life and well.

    There was no one else with whom he had ever needed to treat or bargain.

    He doubted only whether he had made his bribe big
15 enough. God had His price, of course. God was made in man's image, so it had been said: He must have His price.

*iridescent, showing colours like those of the rainbow.

And the price would be rare — no cathedral whose building took many years, no pyramid constructed by ten thousand workmen, would be like this cathedral.

He paused here. That was his proposition. God could
5 take it or leave it.

As he approached the end his sentences became broken, short and uncertain, and his body seemed tense. His hair had qradually turned white as he talked, and now he lifted his head high to the heavens like a prophet of old — magni-
10 ficently mad.

Then, as John stared in fascination, it seemed to him that something curious took place somewhere around him. It was as though the sky had darkened for an instant, as though there had been a sudden murmur in the wind, a
15 sound of far-away trumpets, a sighing. For a time this darkness spread over the land: the birds' song ceased, the trees were still, and far over the mountain there was a sound of dull, menacing thunder.

That was all. The wind died along the tall grasses of the
20 valley. The dawn and the day resumed their place in time, and the risen sun sent hot waves of yellow mist that made its path bright before it. The leaves laughed in the sun, and their laughter shook the trees. God had refused to accept the bribe.

25 For another moment John watched the triumph of the day. Then, turning, he saw the aeroplanes landing one by one like the dance on golden angels alighting from the ·clouds.

John ran down the side of the mountain, where the
30 two girls were awake and waiting for him. They must get off the mountain without losing a moment. He took a hand of each, and in silence they moved among the trees.

When they had gone about half a mile, they avoided the park land and entered a narrow path that led over the
35 next rise of ground. At the highest point of this they turned around and saw clear against the sky a broken, white-haired man slowly coming down the steep slope followed by two

THE DIAMOND AS BIG AS THE RITZ

gigantic and emotionless Negroes, who carried a burden between them which still flashed and glittered in the sun. Half-way down two other figures joined them — John could see that they were Mrs Washington and her son. The aviators had gone from their aeroplanes to the lawn in front of the castle, rifles in hand.

Farther up, Mr Washington and his party stopped by a ledge of rock. The Negroes pulled up what appeared to be a trap-door in the side of the mountain. Into this they all disappeared, the white-haired man first, then his wife and son, and finally the two Negroes.

Kismine clutched John's arm.

'Oh,' she cried wildly, 'where are they going? What are they going to do?'

'It must be some underground way of escape — '

A little scream from the two girls interrupted his sentence.

'Don't you see?' cried Kismine. 'The mountain is wired!'

Before she finished, the whole surface of the mountain had changed suddenly to a bright burning yellow, which showed up through the jacket of turf as light shows through a human hand. For a moment the glow continued, and then was suddenly extinguished, revealing a black waste. Of the aviators there was left neither blood nor bone — they were burnt up as completely as the five souls who had gone inside.

At the same time the castle threw itself into the air, bursting into flame as it rose, and then dropped into the water of the lake. There was no fire. In the air flew a powdery dust of marble that had once been the house of jewels. There was no more sound and the three people were alone in the valley.

The end

At sunset John and his two companions reached the high cliff which had marked the boundaries of the Washingtons' dominion. Looking back they found the valley peaceful and lovely in the dusk. They sat down to finish the food which Jasmine had brought with her in a basket.

'There!' she said, as she spread the tablecloth and put
5   the sandwiches in a neat pile upon it. 'Don't they look tempting? I always think that food tastes better outdoors.'

'Now,' said John eagerly, 'turn out your pockets and let's see what jewels you brought along. If you made a good selection we three ought to live comfortably for the
10   rest of our lives.'

Obediently Kismine put her hand in her pocket and took out two handfuls of glittering stones.

'Not so bad,' cried John, enthusiastically. 'They aren't very big, but — Hello!' His expression changed as he held
15   one of them up to the sun. 'Why, these aren't diamonds! There's something the matter!'

'Oh!' exclaimed Kismine, with surprise. 'What an idiot I am!'

'Why, these are rhinestones*!' cried John.
20   'I know.' She broke into a laugh. 'I opened the wrong drawer. They belonged to a girl who visited Jasmine. I got her to give them to me in exchange for diamonds. I'd never seen anything but precious stones before.'

'And this is what you brought?'
25   'I'm afraid so. I think I like these better. I'm a little tired of diamonds.'

'Very well,' said John gloomily. 'We'll have to live in Hades. And you will grow old telling incredulous women that you got the wrong drawer. Unfortunately your father's
30   bank-books disappeared with him.'

'Well, what's the matter with Hades?'

'If I come home with a wife at my age my father will surely cut me off.'

Jasmine spoke up.
35   'I love washing,' she said quietly. 'I have always washed

---

*rhinestones, worthless imitation gems.

my own handkerchiefs. I'll take in laundry and support you both.'

'Do they have washwomen in Hades?' asked Kismine innocently.

'Of course,' answered John. 'It's just like anywhere else.'   *5*

'I thought — perhaps it was too hot to wear any clothes.'

John laughed.

'Just try it!' he suggested. 'They'll run you out before you're half started.'

'Will father be there?' she asked.   *10*

John turned to her in astonishment.

'Your father is dead,' he replied sombrely. 'Why should he go to Hades? You have it confused with another place which no longer exists.'

After supper they folded up the table-cloth and spread   *15*
their blankets for the night.

'What a dream it was,' Kismine sighed, gazing up at the stars. 'How strange it seems to be here with one dress and a penniless fiancé!'

'Under the stars,' she repeated. 'I never noticed the stars   *20*
before. I always thought of them as great big diamonds that belonged to someone. Now they frighten me. They make me feel that it was all a dream, all my youth.'

'It was a dream,' said John quietly. 'Everybody's youth is a dream, a form of chemical madness.'   *25*

'How pleasant then to be crazy!'

'So I'm told,' said John gloomily.

So wrapping himself in his blanket he fell asleep.

2
Basil: The Freshest* Boy

'You are allowed to go to New York only once a month,'
Lewis Crum was saying, 'and then you have to be accom-
panied by a school master.'
The train was running swiftly past the Indiana countryside.
5 Basil Lee slowly took his eyes away from the fading scenery
in the window to look at his companion.
'I'd just shake him off when I got to New York,' said Basil.
'Yes, you would!' said Lewis Crum sarcastically.
'I bet I would.'
10 'You try it and you'll see!'
'What do you mean by saying I'll see, all the time, Lewis?
What'll I see?'
His very bright dark-blue eyes were at this moment fixed
upon his companion with boredom and impatience. The
15 two had nothing in common except their age, which was
fifteen, and the lifelong friendship of their fathers — which
did not mean much to the boys. Also both of them came
from the same Middle-Western city and were going to the
same school on the East coast not far from New York.
20 It was Basil's first and Lewis's second year at St Regis School.
The thought of having to go back made him quite
miserable. Now he was already homesick for his mother
on whom he had grown very dependent. Lewis hated school.
Basil, on the other hand, had read so many stories of
25 boarding-school life that, far from being homesick, he was
looking forward to it with excitement. Lewis was irritated
by Basil's ignorant enthusiasm and Basil was just as annoyed
by Lewis's attempt to dampen it.
'I'll tell you what you'll see,' he said ominously. 'They'll
30 catch you smoking and put you on bounds*.'

freshest, the most brash. *on bounds*, punishment which takes away the right
to leave school during holidays.

30

'No, they won't, because I won't be smoking. I'll be training for football.'

'Football! Yeah! Football!'

'Honestly, Lewis, you don't like anything, do you?'

'I don't like football. I don't like going out and getting   5
a crack in the eye.' Lewis spoke aggressively.

'You'd probably be a lot more popular in school if you played football,' he suggested patronizingly.

Lewis did not consider himself unpopular. He did not think of it in that way at all. He felt insulted.   10

'You wait!' he cried furiously. 'They'll take all that freshness out of you.'

'Shut up,' said Basil, coolly. 'Just shut up.'

'I guess everybody knows you were the freshest boy at the Country Day!'   15

'Shut up,' repeated Basil, but with less assurance. 'Kindly shut yourself up.'

'I guess I know what they said in the school paper about you — '

Basil was upset by that remark.   20

'If you don't shut up,' he said darkly, 'I'm going to throw your brushes off the train.'

This threat was effective. Lewis sank back in his seat, muttering, but he did not say anymore. What he was referring to was a notice that appeared in the school magazine: 25

If someone will please poison young Basil, or find some other means to stop his mouth, the school at large and myself will be much obliged.

The two boys sat there staring angrily at each other. Basil would like to forget this unpleasant matter of the   30
past. All that was behind him now. Perhaps he had been a little fresh, but he was making a new start.

A letter home

St Regis School,
Eastchester.
November 18, 19 —.

Dear Mother,

5   There is not much to say today, but I thought I
would write to you about my allowance. All the
boys have a bigger allowance than me and there are a
lot of little things I have to get, such as shoe laces, etc.
School is still very nice and I am having a fine time,
10   but football is over and there is not much to do. I am
going to New York this week to see a show. I do not
know yet what it will be, but probably *Quaker
Girl* or *Little Boy Blue* as they are both very good.
Dr Bacon is very nice. No more now as I have to study
15   algebra.

Your affectionate son,

Basil D. Lee.

As he put the letter in its envelope, a little boy came
into the empty study hall where he sat and stood staring at
20   him.
'Hello,' said Basil, frowning.
'I've been looking for you,' said the little boy slowly.
'I looked all over — up in your room and out in the gym,
and they said you had probably sneaked in here.'
25   'What do you want?' Basil demanded.
'Hold your horses, Bossy.'
Basil jumped to his feet. The little boy retreated a step.
'Go on, hit me!' he said nervously. 'Go on, hit me, just
because I'm only half your size — Bossy.'
30   'You call me that again and I'll spank you.'
'No, you won't spank me. Brick Wales said if you ever
touched any of us — '
'Oh, what do you want?' Basil cried in desperation.

'Doctor Bacon wants you. They sent me after you and somebody said maybe you'd sneaked in here.'

Basil dropped his letter in his pocket and walked out. He passed through a long corridor, ascended some stairs and knocked at an ordinary-looking but awe-inspiring door. *5*

The interview

Doctor Bacon was at his desk. He was a handsome, red-headed clergyman of fifty whose attitude was that of all headmasters who have spent half their lives with boys and whose real interest in them has taken a cynical view. Before Basil was asked to sit down, Doctor Bacon took a good look *10* at him through gold-rimmed glasses as if to make sure that he was the right boy. Then he went through the great pile of paper on his desk.

'I had a letter from your mother this morning – ah – Basil.' The use of his first name startled Basil. No one else *15* in school had yet called him anything but Bossy or Lee. 'She feels that your marks have been poor. I believe you have been sent here at a certain amount of – ah – sacrifice and she expects – '

At hearing this, Basil felt ashamed, not at his poor marks *20* but that he should be reminded so bluntly of his not so well-to-do family background. He knew that he was one of the poorest boys in a rich boys' school.

Perhaps Doctor Bacon became aware of his discomfort; he shuffled through the papers once more and began on *25* a new note.

'However, that is not why I sent for you this afternoon. You applied last week for permission to go to New York on Saturday, to see a performance. Mr Davis tells me that for the first time since school opened you will be off bounds *30* tomorrow.'

'Yes, sir.'

'That is not a good record. However, I would allow you to

33

go to New York if it could be arranged. Unfortunately, no masters are available this Saturday.'

Basil's mouth dropped. 'Why, I — why, Doctor Bacon, I know two parties that are going. Couldn't I go with one of them?' 5

Doctor Bacon ran through all his papers very quickly. 'Unfortunately, one is composed of slightly older boys and the other group made arrangements some weeks ago.'

'How about the party that's going to *Quaker Girl* with Mr Dunn?' 10

'It's that party I speak of. They feel that the arrangements are completed and they have bought seats together.'

Suddenly Basil understood from the look in his eye. Doctor Bacon went on hurriedly, 'There's perhaps one thing I can do. Of course there must be several boys in the party so 15 that the master's expenses can be divided up amongst all. If you can find two other boys who would like to make up a party, and let me have their names by five o'clock, I'll send Mr Rooney with you.'

'Thank you,' said Basil. 20

Doctor Bacon hesitated. He wanted to find out what made Basil the most unpopular boy in the school. Both teachers and pupils shared the same extraordinary dislike for him. Doctor Bacon was unable to find the cause of this even with the help of other sixth form students. It was probably a 25 question of personality.

He sighed. Sometimes these things worked themselves out. He wasn't one to try to interfere. 'Let us have a better report to send home next month, Basil.'

'Yes, sir.' 30

Basil ran quickly downstairs to the recreation room. It was Wednesday and most of the boys had already gone into the nearby village. When he looked at those still scattered about the pool tables and piano, he saw that it was going to be difficult to get anyone to go with him at all. For 35 Basil was quite aware that he was the most unpopular boy at school.

It had begun almost immediately. One day, less than a fortnight after he came, a crowd of the smaller boys suddenly gathered around him and began calling him Bossy. Within the next week he had two fights, and both times the crowd
5   sided with the other boy. He joined a group innocently at the piano and was told, 'Go away! We don't want you around.'

After a month he began to realize how unpopular he was. It shocked him. One day after a particularly bitter humilia-
10 tion he went up to his room and cried. He tried to keep out of the way for a while, but it didn't help. He was accused of sneaking off here and there, as if he was plotting something bad in secret. Puzzled and unhappy, he looked at his face in the glass, trying to discover the secret of their
15 dislike in the expression of his eyes, his smile.

He saw now that in certain ways he had annoyed the boys. He had boasted. He had been considered a coward at football. He had pointed out people's mistakes to them. He had showed off his general information in class. But
20 he had tried to do better and couldn't understand why he had failed. It was too late now. He would be unpopular forever.

He had, indeed, become the scapegoat, and the target of all unkindness. His self-confidence was entirely broken.

This trip to New York had become very important to
25 him. It would mean an escape from the misery of his daily life as well as a glimpse into the long-waited heaven of romance. Its postponement for week after week due to his misconduct had deepened his longing until it was a burning hunger. He was desperate to find someone to go with him,
30 even if it meant breaking bounds. There were Fat Gaspar, Treadway, and Bugs Brown whom he could ask to accompany him. On this Wednesday afternoon he knew they had gone to Eastchester. He put on his cap against the chilly November wind, and set out along the half-mile road to
35 town.

36

Eastchester

Eastchester was a suburban farming community, with a small shoe factory. There were three places there he was sure to run into the boys he wanted to find. He tried a snack bar known as 'The Dog' first, and found Bugs Brown there. 5

Bugs Brown was a hysterical boy and was considered by the other boys as mad because he had the nervous habit of making strange sounds all day long.

When Basil came in, he was in the company of several younger boys. 10

'Who-ee!' he cried. 'Ee-ee-ee!' He put his hand over his mouth making these sounds. 'It's Bossy Lee! It's Boss-Boss-Boss-Boss-Boss Lee!'

'Wait a minute, Bugs,' said Basil anxiously, 'Don't! Wait a minute! Can you come up to New York this Saturday 15 afternoon?'

'Whe-ee-ee!' cried Bugs to Basil's distress. 'Wee-ee-ee!'

'Honestly, Bugs, tell me, can you? We could go up together if you could go.'

'I've got to see a doctor,' said Bugs, suddenly calm. 'He 20 wants to see how crazy I am.'

'Can't you see about it some other day?' said Basil.

'Whee-ee-ee!' cried Bugs.

'All right then,' said Basil hastily. 'Have you seen Fat Gasper in town?' 25

Basil was directed to the 'Bostonian Candy Kitchen'.

The place smelled like a cheap candy factory. Inside, a line of boys sat eating heavy dinners of banana splits, and chocolate-marshmallow nut sundaes. Basil found Fat Gasper at a table at the side. 30

Fat Gasper was considered a nice fellow — in fact he was so pleasant that he had been courteous to Basil. Basil realized that he was like that to everyone, yet it was just possible that Fat liked him. In any case, he was so desperate that he was willing to take a chance. But as he approached the 35 table and saw the unfriendly faces that turned to him, his hope diminished.

'Say, Fat — ' he said, and hesitated. Then he burst forth suddenly. 'I'm on bounds, but I ran off because I had to see
5 you. Doctor Bacon told me I could go to New York on Saturday if I could get two other boys to go. I asked Bugs Brown and he couldn't go, and I thought I'd ask you.'

He broke off, extremely embarrassed, and waited. Suddenly the two boys with Fat burst into howls of laughter.
10 'Bugs wasn't crazy enough!'

Fat Gasper hesitated. He couldn't go to New York on Saturday and ordinarily he would have refused without offending. He had nothing against Basil; but he was conscious of what the other boys would think of him.
15 'I don't want to go,' he said. 'Why are you asking me?'

Then, half in shame, he gave a little laugh and bent over his ice-cream.

'I just thought I'd ask you,' said Basil.

Turning away quickly, he went to the counter and in
20 a hollow and unfamiliar voice ordered a strawberry sundae. He ate it mechanically, hearing occasional whispers and sniggers from the table behind. Still feeling confused, he started to walk out without paying his check, but the clerk called him back and he was conscious of more people
25 laughing at him.

For a moment he wondered whether to go back to the table and hit one of them in the face, but he saw nothing to be gained from doing that. They would tell the truth — that he had done it because he couldn't get anybody to go
30 to New York. Angry but unable to do anything, he walked out of the store.

Immediately he came upon his third chance. Treadway. Treadway had entered St Regis late in the year and had been put in the same room as Basil the week before. Their
35 relations, if not close, had at least been peaceful.

'Hey, Treadway,' he called, still excited from what had happened a moment ago, 'can you come up to New York

38

to a show on Saturday afternoon?'

He stopped, realizing that Treadway was in the company of Brick Wales, a boy he had had a fight with and who was one of his bitterest enemies. Looking from one to the other, Basil saw a look of impatience in Treadway's face and a fara- 5
way expression in Brick Wales's. He realized that Brick Wales must have told the new boy how unpopular his room-mate was. Treadway preferred to stop being friendly.

'Not on your life,' he said briefly. 'So long.' The two walked past him into the Candy Kitchen. 10

He had got quite used to these slights. If they had happened to him at the beginning of term, he would have been shattered. Still his pride was hurt, and he had to try not to cry.

On the way back to school, he heard footsteps approaching 15
and he stood motionless, afraid to be caught by any of the masters. Their voices grew nearer and louder; before he knew it he was listening:

' — so after he tried Bugs Brown, the poor fool asked Fat Gasper to go with him and Fat said, "Why are you asking 20
me?" It would serve him right if he couldn't get anybody at all.'

It was the triumphant voice of Lewis Crum.

Back in his room, Basil was very tempted to have a good cry by himself. He controlled himself as he heard Treadway 25
come in, but did not look up. He listened as Treadway moved about the room, and after a while he became conscious that there was an unusual opening of closets and drawers. Basil turned over, his arm hiding his tear-stained face. Treadway had an armful of shirts in his hand. 30

'What are you doing?' Basil demanded.

His room-mate looked at him stonily. 'I'm moving in with Wales,' he said.

'Oh!'

Treadway went on with his packing. He carried out a 35
full suitcase, then another, took down some pennants and dragged his trunk into the hall. Basil watched him bundle

his toilet things into a towel and take one last look to see if he had forgotten anything.

'Good-bye,' he said to Basil, without a ripple of emotion in his voice.

5   'Good-bye.'

Treadway went out. Basil turned over once more and choked into the pillow.

'Oh, poor baby!' he cried huskily. 'Poor little baby! Poor little baby!'

New York

10   Doctor Bacon, who realized how miserable Basil must have felt, arranged that he should go to New York, after all. He went, in the company of Mr Rooney, the football coach and history teacher. At twenty Mr Rooney had hesitated for some time between joining the police force
15   and going to college. In fact he did not make a very good teacher and Doctor Bacon was planning to get rid of him at Christmas. Mr Rooney disliked Basil for his unreliable conduct on the football field during the past season; he had consented to take him to New York for reasons of his own.
20   Basil sat meekly beside him on the train, glancing at the fields outside. Mr Rooney finished his newspaper, folded it up and sank into a moody silence. He remembered that Basil was a fresh boy, and that he was so quiet now annoyed him.

25   'Lee,' he said suddenly, with a little friendly interest, 'why don't you get wise to yourself?'

'What, sir?' Basil was startled from his excited trance of this morning.

'I said why don't you get wise to yourself?' said Mr
30   Rooney in a somewhat violent tone. 'Do you want to be the butt of the school all your time here?'

'No, I don't,' Basil was chilled. 'Couldn't all this be left behind for just one day?'

'You oughtn't to get so fresh all the time. A couple of times in history class I could just about have broken your neck.' Basil could think of no appropriate answer. 'Then out playing football,' continued Mr Rooney, ' — you didn't 5
have any nerve. You could play better than a lot of them if you wanted, like that day against the Pomfret Seconds, but you lost your nerve.'

'I shouldn't have tried for the second team,' said Basil. 'I was too light. I should have stayed in the third.' 10

'You are a coward, that is the trouble. You ought to get wise to yourself. In class, you're always thinking of something else. If you don't study, you'll never get to college.'

'I'm the youngest boy in the fifth form.' Basil said rashly.

'You think you're pretty bright, don't you?' He eyed 15
Basil ferociously. Then something seemed to occur to him that changed his attitude and they rode for a while in silence. When the train began to run through the thickly clustered communities near New York, he spoke again in a milder voice and with an air of having considered the matter for 20
a long time:

'Lee, I'm going to trust you.'

'Yes, sir.'

'You go and get some lunch and then go on to your show. I've got some business of my own I've got to attend 25
to, and when I've finished I'll try to get to the show. If I can't, I'll meet you outside.' Basil's heart leaped. 'Yes, sir.'

'I don't want you to open your mouth about this at school — I mean, about my doing some business of my own.'

'No, sir.' 30

'We'll see if you can keep your mouth shut for once,' he said, making it fun. Then he added sternly, 'And no drinks, you understand that?'

'Oh, no, sir!' The idea shocked Basil. He had never tasted a drink, nor ever thought that he would. 35

THE DIAMOND AS BIG AS THE RITZ AND OTHER STORIES

On his own in New York

On the advice of Mr Rooney he went for luncheon to the
Manhattan Hotel, near the station, where he ordered a
club sandwich, French fried potatoes, and a chocolate
parfait. He sat there watching the stylish New Yorkers at
5 the other tables dreamily. School had fallen from him like
a burden. He even delayed opening the letter from the
morning's mail which he found in his pocket, because it
was addressed to him at school.

He wanted another chocolate parfait, but being reluctant
10 to bother the busy waiter any more, he opened the letter and
spread it before him instead. It was from his mother.

Dear Basil,

This is written in great haste, as I didn't want to
frighten you by telegraphing. Grandfather is going
15 abroad and he wants you and me to come too. The
idea is that you'll go to school at Grenoble or Montreux
for the rest of the year and learn French and we'll be
close by. That is, if you want to. I know how you like
St Regis and playing football and baseball, and of
20 course there would be none of that; but on the other
hand, it would be a nice change, even if it postponed
your entering Yale by an extra year. So, as usual, I
want you to do just as you like. We will be leaving
home almost as soon as you get this and will come
25 to the Waldorf in New York, where you can come
in and see us for a few days, even if you decide to
stay. Think it over, dear.

With love to my dearest boy,

Mother.

30 Basil got up from his chair with an idea of walking over
to the Waldorf and locking himself in safely until his mother
came. No more St Regis! No more St Regis! He was almost
overcome with happiness.

42

'Oh, gosh!' he cried to himself. 'Oh, golly! Oh, gosh! Oh, gosh!' No more Doctor Bacon and Mr Rooney and Brick Wales and Fat Gasper. He need no longer hate them, for they were just shadows, sliding past.

At the theatre

It required the noise of Forty-second Street to make 5
him sober again. With his hand on his purse to guard against pickpockets, he moved cautiously towards Broadway. What a day! He would tell Mr Rooney — Why, he needn't ever go back! Or perhaps it would be better to go back and let them know what he was going to do, while *they* went 10
on and on in the dismal, dreary round of school.

He found the theatre and entered the lobby. As he took out his ticket, his gaze was caught and held by a familiar face a few feet away. It was that of a well-built, blond, young man of about twenty with a strong chin and direct grey 15
eyes. What a day! He had never actually seen the young man before, but from a thousand pictures he knew that it was Ted Fay, the Yale football captain, who had, almost single-handed, beaten Harvard and Princeton last fall*. To any school-boy who cared about football, he was a hero, 20
a legend, a sign in the sky. The crowd revolved; the hero disappeared. But Basil would know all through the next hours that Ted Fay was here too.

In the darkness of the theatre he read the programme. It was the show of all shows that he wanted to see, and 25
until the curtain actually rose the programme itself had a curious sacredness. But when the curtain rose it became waste paper to be dropped carelessly to the floor.

It was too bright and blinding to understand what was going on in the first act of the show. It went so fast that 30
from the very first Basil felt he had missed things. He would make his mother take him again when she came next week.

fall, autumn.

43

An hour passed. In a blaze of light and sound, the first two acts were over.

Still lingering in his ear was the refrain of the song:

'Rose — Rose — Rose of the night,

5   When the spring moon is bright you'll be fair — '

A few minutes later, feeling oddly shaken and excited, Basil drifted outside with the crowd. The first thing that his eyes fell upon was the almost forgotten Mr Rooney.

Mr Rooney had, in fact, gone a little to pieces. He was,
10   to begin with, wearing a different and much smaller hat than when he left Basil at noon. Secondly, his face had turned quite white, his necktie was undone and even his shirt was hanging over his pants. How, in the short space of four hours, Mr Rooney had got himself in such shape was difficult
15   to understand.

'Aren't you coming to the show?' he asked, even though Mr Rooney was not in any condition to come to the show.

Mr Rooney took off his hat. His hair was all wet.

'We've got to get back to school,' he said in an uncon-
20   vincing voice.

'But there's another act,' protested Basil in horror. 'I've got to stay for the last act.'

'All right,' he agreed. 'I'm going to get something to eat. I'll wait for you next door.'

25   Half an hour passed. Basil went into the lobby and stood in thought while the crowd passed out. His mother's letter and the show had cleared his mind of all his unhappiness — he was his old self and he wanted to do the right thing. He wondered if it was the right thing to get Mr Rooney back
30   to school. He walked towards the saloon. Mr Rooney was sound asleep at a table in the back of the room.

Not knowing what to do, he went outside to think. He would give Mr Rooney half an hour. If, at the end of that time, he had not come out, he would go back to school.
35   After all, Mr Rooney had been giving him a bad time ever since the football season. Basil was simply washing his hands of the whole affair as in a day or so he would wash

44

his hands of school.

He had taken several turns up and down the sidewalk, when glancing up an alley that ran beside the theatre his eye was caught by the sign, Stage Entrance. He could watch the actors come out.   5

Basil follows

He waited. Suddenly a girl came out and with her a man. Basil turned and ran a few steps up the street as if afraid they would recognize him. He ran back breathing as if he had had a heart attack. The girl was a radiant little beauty of nineteen. She was the star of the show and the young   10
man by her side was Ted Fay.

Arm in arm, they walked past him, and Basil followed. As they walked, she leaned towards Ted Fay in a way that showed intimacy. They crossed Broadway and turned into the Knickerbocker Hotel, and twenty feet behind them   15
Basil followed, in time to see them go into a long room set for afternoon tea. They sat at a table for two, spoke vaguely to a waiter, and then, alone at last, bent eagerly towards each other. Basil saw that Ted Fay was holding her gloved hand.   20

Basil sat down at a table next to them behind a row of potted plants.

Her voice was low and less certain than it had been in the play, and very sad: 'Of course I do, Ted.' For a long time, as their conversation continued, she repeated, 'Of   25
course I do' or 'But I do, Ted.' Ted Fay's remarks were too low for Basil to hear.

' — says next month, and he won't be put off any more . . . I do in a way, Ted. It's hard to explain, but he's done everything for mother and me . . . There's no use kidding myself.   30
It was a part that couldn't go wrong and any girl he gave it to would become a star overnight. He's been awfully thoughtful. He's done everything for me.'

Basil's ears were sharpened by the intensity of her emotion;
now he could hear Ted Fay's voice too:

'And you say you love me.'

'But don't you see I promised to marry him more than
5 a year ago.'

'Tell him the truth — that you love me. Ask him to let
you off.'

'This isn't musical comedy, Ted.'

'That was a mean one,' he said bitterly.

10 'I'm sorry, dear, Ted darling, but you're driving me crazy
going on this way. You're making it so hard for me.'

'I'm going to leave New Haven, anyhow.'

'No, you're not. You're going to stay and play football
this spring. You're an ideal to all those boys! Why, if you — '

15 He laughed shortly. 'You're a fine one to talk about ideals.'

'Why not? I'm living up to my responsibility to Beltzman;

you've got to make up your mind just like I have — that we can't have each other.'

'Jerry! Think what you're doing! All my life, whenever I hear that waltz — '

Basil got to his feet and hurried down the corridor, *5* through the lobby and out of the hotel. He was in a state of wild emotional confusion. He did not understand all he had heard, but he had gathered that life for everybody was a struggle, sometimes magnificent from a distance, but always difficult and surprisingly simple and a little sad. *10*

They would go on. Ted Fay would go back to Yale, put her picture in his drawer and play football this spring. For her at 8.30 the curtain would go up and she would miss something warm and young out of her life, something she had had this afternoon. *15*

A decision

It was dark outside and Broadway was a blazing forest fire as Basil walked slowly along towards the point of brightest light. He would see it a lot now, he would come whenever he could get off from school.

5   But that was all changed — he was going to Europe. Suddenly Basil realized that he wasn't going to Europe. The conquest of the successive worlds of school, college and New York — why, that was his true dream that he had carried from boyhood into adolescence. He was not to

10   give it up and run away first because of a few boys who laughed at him. He shivered violently, like a dog coming out of the water, and at the same time, he was reminded of Mr Rooney.

A few minutes later he walked into the bar, and up to the

15   table where Mr Rooney still sat asleep. Basil shook him gently, then firmly. Mr Rooney stirred and saw Basil.

'Get wise to yourself,' he muttered drowsily. 'Get wise to yourself and let me alone.'

'I am wise to myself,' said Basil. 'Honest, I am wise to

20   myself, Mr Rooney. You've got to come with me into the washroom and get cleaned up, and then you can sleep on the train again, Mr Rooney. Come on, Mr Rooney, please — '

It was a long hard term. Basil was on bounds again in December and wasn't free again until March. He made

25   countless new starts, failed and tried again.

He made friends with a new boy named Maplewood after Christmas, but they had a silly quarrel; and through the winter term, Basil was snubbed and slighted a good deal for his real and imaginary sins, and he was much alone.

30   But on the other hand, there was Ted Fay, and Rose of the Night singing — 'All my life whenever I hear that waltz' — and he remembered the lights of New York, and he thought of the glamorous image of Yale and the hope of spring in the air.

35   Fat Gaspar and a few others were nice to him now. Once

when he and Fat walked home together by accident from downtown they had a long talk about something of common interest. Basil was wise enough not to try to sound too clever. The smaller boys suddenly decided that they approved of him, and a master who had previously disliked him put   5 his hand on his shoulder walking to a class one day. They would all forget eventually — maybe during the summer. There would be new fresh boys in September; he would have a clean start next year.

One afternoon in February, playing basketball, a great   10 thing happened. He and Brick Wales were at forward on the second team and everyone was crying at the top of their voices in moments of excitement.

'Here yar!'

'Bill! Bill!'   15

Basil had dribbled the ball down the court and Brick Wales, free, was crying for it.

'Here yar! Lee! Hey! Lee-y!'

Lee-y!

Basil flushed and made a poor pass. He had been called   20 by a nickname which was not abusive. Brick Wales went on playing, unconscious that he had done anything in particular or that he had saved him from the unhappy fate of being the most unpopular boy.

Lee-y! It could scarcely be pronounced. But Basil took   25 it to bed with him that night and thinking of it, holding it to him happily to the last, fell easily asleep.

3
Babylon Revisited

'And where's Mr Campbell?'

'Gone to Switzerland. Mr Campbell's a pretty sick man, Mr Wales.'

'I'm sorry to hear that. And George Hardt?' Charlie asked.

5 'Back in America.'

'And where is the Snow Bird?'

'He was in here last week. Anyway, his friend, Mr Schaeffer, is in Paris.'

Two familiar names from the past. Charlie quickly wrote 10 down an address in his notebook and tore out the page.

'If you see Mr Schaeffer, give him this,' he said. 'It's my brother-in-law's address. I haven't decided which hotel to stay in yet.'

He was not really disappointed to find Paris was so empty. 15 He felt the stillness from the moment he got out of the taxi and saw the doorman, usually very busy at this hour, gossiping with a bell-hop* by the servants' entrance.

Standing at the bar, he looked around the room. Nobody seemed to pay him any attention, except someone in a 20 corner who looked up once from a newspaper.

The bartender, Alix, asked if he would like to have another drink.

'No, no more,' Charlie said. 'I'm slowing down these days.'

25 'I remember that you never refused a drink two years ago!' Alix said.

'Well, I'm a new man now,' Charlie answered.

'How do you find conditions in America?'

'I haven't been to America for months. I'm in business 30 in Prague. They don't know about me there.'

Alix smiled.

*bell-hop, a hotel worker.

50

'How long are you going to stay here, Mr Wales?'

'I'm here for four or five days to see my little girl.'

Outside, signs in different colours shone through the rain. It was late afternoon and the streets were busy. He took a taxi. *5*

Charlie directed his taxi to the Avenue of the Opera, which was out of his way. But he wanted to see the wonderful Opera House in the evening light again. On his way he saw people going to dinner in the restaurants. He had never eaten at a really cheap restaurant in Paris. For some odd *10* reason he wished that he had.

'I spoiled this city for myself,' he thought. 'I didn't realize it, but the days came along one after another, and then two years were gone, and everything was gone, and I was gone.'

The visit

He was thirty-five and good-looking. There was a deep *15* line between his eyes which gave his lively face a serious look. As he rang his brother-in-law's door-bell, he felt very nervous. When the door opened, a lovely little girl of nine ran out from behind the maid, shouting at the top of her voice, 'Daddy!' She flew into his arms, pulled his head *20* around by one ear and put her cheek against his.

'My old pie,' he said.

'Oh, daddy, daddy, daddy, daddy, dads, dads, dads!'

She drew him into the room, where the family waited; a boy and a girl his daughter's age, his sister-in-law and *25* her husband. He greeted Marion with a voice that showed neither enthusiasm nor dislike. She, Marion, was not particularly pleased to see him. In order not to display her distrust for him, she turned her attention to his child. The two men shook hands in a friendly way and Lincoln *30* Peters rested his hand for a moment on Charlie's shoulder.

The room was warm and comfortable. The three children moved about, playing. The fire and sounds of cooking in the kitchen added to the homely atmosphere of the place. But Charlie did not relax. He drew confidence from his daughter, who from time to time came close to him, holding in her arms the doll he had brought.

5 'Really extremely well,' he said in answer to Lincoln's question. 'There's a lot of business there that isn't moving at all, but we're doing even better than ever. In fact, very well. I'm bringing my sister over from America next month to keep house for me. My income last year was bigger than

10 it was when I had money. You see.'

He had a reason to boast; but after a moment, seeing a faint uneasiness in Lincoln's eyes, he changed the subject: 'Those are fine children of yours, well brought up, good manners.'

15 'We think Honoria's a great little girl too.'

Marion Peters came back from the kitchen. She was a tall woman with worried eyes, who had once possessed a fresh loveliness. Charlie had never been sensitive to it and was always surprised when people spoke of how pretty

20 she had been. From the first there had been a dislike between them.

'Well, how do you find Honoria?' she asked.

'Wonderful. I was astonished how much she's grown in ten months. All the children are looking well.'

25 'We haven't had a doctor for a year. How do you like being back in Paris?'

'It seems very funny to see so few Americans around.'

'I'm delighted,' Marion said with a strong feeling. 'Now at least you can go into a store without their thinking you're

30 a millionaire. We've suffered like everybody, but on the whole it's a good deal pleasanter.'

'But it was nice while it lasted,' Charlie said. 'We were a sort of royalty*, with a sort of magic around us. In the bar this afternoon — ' he hesitated, seeing his mistake,

35 'there wasn't a man I knew.'

She looked at him sharply. 'I should think you'd have

*royalty, members of the royal family.

had enough of bars.'

'I only stayed a minute. I take one drink every afternoon, and no more.'

'Don't you want one before dinner?' Lincoln asked.

'I take only one drink every afternoon, and I've had that.'   5

'I hope you keep to it,' said Marion.

Her dislike was shown in the coldness with which she spoke, but Charlie only smiled. He had bigger plans. Her very aggressiveness gave him an advantage, and he knew enough to wait. He wanted them to bring up the discussion   10
of what they knew had brought him to Paris.

At dinner he couldn't decide whether Honoria was most like him or her mother. He felt very protective towards her. He thought he knew what to do for her.

He left soon after dinner, but not to go home. He was   15
curious to see Paris by night with clearer eyes than those of other days. He went to the Casino to watch a dance performance.

After an hour he left and strolled towards Montmartre*. The rain had stopped and there were a few people in evening   20
clothes getting out of taxis in front of night-clubs. He went past clubs and cafes where he had passed so many hours and parted with so much money in his days of dissipation*, and he suddenly realised that he had wasted a great deal of things precious to life.   25

He remembered thousand-franc notes given to an orchestra for playing a song, hundred-franc notes given to a doorman for calling a cab.

But it hadn't been given for nothing. It had been given, as an offering to destiny that he might not remember the things   30
most worth remembering, the things that now he would always remember — his child taken from his control, his wife escaped to a grave in Vermont.

---

*Montmartre, an area in Paris well-know for its places of entertainment. *dissipation, an unproductive way of spending one's time, energy or money.

The next day

He woke upon a fine day — football weather. The depression of yesterday was gone and he liked the people on the streets. At noon he had lunch with Honoria at Vatel, the only restaurant that would not remind him of the past.

5 'Now, how about vegetables? Oughtn't you to have some vegetables?'

'Well, yes.'

'There's spinach and cauliflower and carrots and green beans.'

10 'I'd like cauliflower.'

'Wouldn't you like to have two vegetables?'

'I usually only have one at lunch.'

'How about dessert? Shall we wait and see?'

Honoria looked at her father expectantly.

15 'What are we going to do?'

'First, we're going to that toy store to buy you anything you like. And then we're going to a show at the Empire.'

She hesitated. 'I like the idea of going to a show, but not the toy store.'

20 'Why not?'

'Well, you brought me this doll.' She had it with her. 'And I've got lots of things. And we're not rich any more, are we?'

'We never were. But today you are to have anything you 25 want.'

'All right,' she agreed resignedly.

When there had been her mother and a French nurse he was inclined to be strict; now that he must be both parents to her he became more tolerant.

30 'I want to get to know you,' he said gravely. 'First let me introduce myself. My name is Charles J. Wales, of Prague.'

'Oh, daddy!' her voice cracked with laughter.

'And who are you, please?' he asked.

'Honoria Wales, Rue Palatine, Paris.'

35 'Married or single?'

'No, not married. Single.'

He pointed to the doll. 'But I see you have a child, madam.'

She took it to her heart and thought quickly: 'Yes, I've been married, but I'm not married now. My husband is   5
dead.'

He went on quickly, 'And the child's name?'

'Simone. That's after my best friend at school.'

'I'm very pleased that you're doing so well at school.'

'I was third this month,' she boasted. 'Elsie (that was   10
her cousin) is only about eighteenth, and Richard is about
at the bottom.'

'You like Richard and Elsie, don't you?'

'Oh, yes. I like Richard quite well and I like her all right.'

Carefully and casually he asked: 'And Aunt Marion and   15
Uncle Lincoln — which do you like best?'

'Oh, Uncle Lincoln, I guess.'

'Why don't I live with you?' she asked suddenly. 'Because
mamma's dead?'

'You must stay here and learn more French. It would   20
have been hard for daddy to take care of you so well.'

'I don't really need much taking care of any more. I do
everything for myself.'

Going out of the restaurant, a man and a woman unex-
pectedly called out to him.   25

'Well, it's old Wales!'

'Hello there, Lorraine .... Dunc.'

Sudden ghosts out of the past: Duncan Schaeffer, a
friend from college. Lorraine Quarrles, a lovely, pale blonde
of thirty; one of a crowd who had helped them make months   30
into days in the lavish times of three years ago.

'This your little girl?' she asked.

'What about coming back and sitting down?' Duncan
asked.

'Can't do it.' He was glad for an excuse.   35

'Well, how about dinner?' she asked.

'I'm not free. Give me your address and let me call you.'

Charlie pointed to Honoria with his head. They both laughed.

'What's your address?' said Duncan.

He hesitated, unwilling to give the name of his hotel.

5 'I'm not settled yet. I'd better call you. We're going to see the show at the Empire.'

'There! That's what I want to do,' Lorraine said. 'I want to see some clowns and acrobats and jugglers. That's just what we'll do, Dunc.'

10 'We've got to do something first,' said Charlie. 'Perhaps we'll see you there.'

'All right, you snob . . . Good-bye, beautiful little girl.'

'Good-bye.'

Honoria nodded politely.

15 Somehow, an unwelcome encounter. They liked him because he was serious; they wanted to see him, because he was stronger than they were now, because they wanted to draw from his strength.

At the Empire, Honoria proudly refused to sit upon 20 her father's folded coat. She was already an individual with a mind of her own, and Charlie more and more wanted to put a little of himself into her before she was fully grown. It was hopeless to try to know her in so short a time.

Between the acts they came upon Duncan and Lorraine 25 in the lobby where the band was playing.

'Have a drink?'

'All right, but not up at the bar. We'll take a table.'

'The perfect father.'

Only half listening to Lorraine, Charlie watched Honoria's 30 eyes leave their table, and he followed them about the room, wondering what they saw. He met her glance and she smiled. 'I liked that lemonade,' she said.

What had she said? What had he expected? Going home in a taxi afterwards, he pulled her over until her head rested 35 against his chest.

'Darling, do you ever think about your mother?'

'Yes, sometimes,' she answered vaguely.

'I don't want you to forget her. Have you got a picture of her?'

'Yes, I think so. Anyhow, Aunt Marion has. Why don't you want me to forget her?'

'She loved you very much.'   5

'I loved her too.'

They were silent for a moment.

'Daddy, I want to come and live with you,' she said suddenly.

His heart jumped; he had wanted it to come like this.   10

'Aren't you perfectly happy?'

'Yes, but I love you better than anybody. And you love me better than anybody, don't you, now that mummy's dead?'

'Of course I do. But you won't always like me best,   15
honey. You'll grow up and meet somebody your own age and go marry him and forget you ever had a daddy.'

'Yes, that's true,' she agreed calmly.

He didn't go in. He was coming back at nine o'clock and he wanted to keep himself fresh and new for the thing   20
he must say then.

'When you're safe inside, just show yourself in that window.'

'All right. Good-bye, dads, dads, dads, dads.'

He waited in the dark street until she appeared, all warm 25
and glowing, in the window above and kissed her fingers out into the night.

The future

They were waiting. Marion sat there in a black dinner dress that just faintly suggested mourning. Lincoln was walking up and down. They were as anxious as he was   30
to get into the question. He opened the conversation almost immediately:

'I suppose you know what I want to see you about —

57

why I really came to Paris.'

Marion frowned.

'I'm very anxious to have a home,' he continued. 'And I'm anxious to have Honoria in it. I appreciate your taking in Honoria for her mother's sake, but things have changed now and I want to ask you to reconsider the matter. It would be silly for me to deny that about three years ago I was acting badly — '

' — but all that's over. As I told you, I haven't had more than a drink a day for over a year. Anyhow, I couldn't afford to drink in my position. The people I represent are more than satisfied with what I've done, I'm bringing my sister over from Burlington to keep house for me, and I want very much to have Honoria too. You know that even when her mother and I weren't getting along well we never let anything that happened touch Honoria. I know she's fond of me and I know I'm able to take care of her and — well, there you are. How do you feel about it?'

He knew that now he would have to take a beating. It would last an hour or two hours, and it would be difficult, but, he might win his point in the end.

Keep your temper, he told himself. You don't want to be justified. You want Honoria.

Lincoln spoke first: 'We've been talking it over since we got your letter last month. We're happy to have Honoria here. She's a dear little thing, and we're glad to be able to help her, but of course that isn't the question.'

Marion interrupted suddenly. 'How long are you going to stay sober, Charlie?' she asked.

'Permanently, I hope.'

'How can anybody count on that?'

'You know I never did drink heavily until I gave up business and came over here with nothing to do. Then Helen and I began to run around with . . . '

'Please leave Helen out of it. I can't bear to hear you talk about her like that.'

He stared at her grimly. He had never been certain how

fond of each other the sisters were in life.

'My drinking only lasted about a year and a half — from the time we came over until I — collapsed.'

'It was time enough.'

'It was time enough,' he agreed. 5

'My duty is entirely to Helen,' she said. 'I try to think what she would have wanted me to do. Frankly, from the night you did that terrible thing you haven't really existed for me. I can't help that. She was my sister.'

'Yes.' 10

'When she was dying she asked me to look after Honoria. If you hadn't been in a sanatorium then, it might have helped matters.'

He had no answer.

'I'll never in my life be able to forget the morning when 15 Helen knocked at my door, wet and shivering, and said you'd locked her out.'

Charlie gripped the sides of the chair. This was more difficult than he expected; he wanted to explain, but he only said: 'The night I locked her out — ' and she inter- 20 rupted, 'I don't feel up to going over that again.'

After a moment's silence Lincoln said: 'We're getting off the subject. You want Marion to set aside her legal guardianship* and give you Honoria. I think the main point for her is whether she has confidence in you or not.' 25

'I don't blame Marion,' Charlie said slowly, 'but I think she can have entire confidence in me. I had a good record up to three years ago. Of course, it's within human possibilities I might go wrong any time. But if we wait much longer I'll lose Honoria's childhood and my chance for a home.' He shook 30 his head, 'I'll simply lose her, don't you see?'

'Yes, I see,' said Lincoln.

'Why didn't you think of all this before?' Marion asked.

'I suppose I did, from time to time, but Helen and I were getting along badly. When I consented to the guardianship, 35 I was in a sanatorium and the market had cleaned me out.

*legal guardianship, the right, by law, to look after a young person.

59

But now it's different. I'm working again, I'm behaving damn well, so far as . . . '

'Please don't swear at me,' Marion said.

He looked at her, surprised. The force of her dislike
5 became more and more clear. She had built up all her fear of life against him. Charlie became increasingly alarmed at leaving Honoria in this atmosphere of unfriendliness towards him. Sooner or later it would come out in a word here, a shake of the head there, and some of that distrust
10 would be put in Honoria. But he controlled his temper. He had won a point, for Lincoln realized the unreasonableness of Marion's remark and asked her lightly since when she had objected to the word 'damn'.

'Another thing,' Charlie said, 'I'm going to get someone
15 to look after her, and I have rented a new apartment.'

He stopped, realizing that he was saying the wrong things. They couldn't be expected to accept the fact that his income was again twice as large as their own.

'I suppose you can give her more luxuries than we can,'
20 said Marion. 'When you were throwing away money we were existing, watching every ten francs. . . I suppose you'll start doing it again.'

'Oh, no,' he said. 'I've learned. I worked hard for ten years, you know — until I got lucky in the market, like so
25 many people. Terribly lucky. It won't happen again.'

There was a long silence. He was sure now that Lincoln Peters wanted him to have his child.

Marion shuddered suddenly; part of her saw that Charlie's feet were planted on the earth now, and her own feeling
30 of a mother recognized the naturalness of his desire; but she had lived for a long time with a dislike for him.

'I can't help what I think!' she cried out suddenly. 'How much you were responsible for Helen's death, I don't know. It's something you'll have to answer for yourself.'

35 For a moment he felt too much pain to speak. He held on to himself for a moment, another moment.

'Hold on there,' said Lincoln uncomfortably. 'I never

thought you were responsible for that.'

'Helen died of heart trouble,' Charlie said dully.

'Yes, heart trouble.' Marion spoke as if the phrase had another meaning for her.

Then, she knew he was somehow in control of the situation. Glancing at her husband, she found no help from him.

'Do what you like!' she cried, springing up from her chair. 'She's your child. I'm not the person to stand in your way. I think if it were my child I'd rather see her . . . ' She managed to stop herself. 'You two decide. I can't stand this, I'm sick. I'm going to bed.'

She hurried from the room; after a moment Lincoln said:

'This has been a hard day for her. You know how strongly she feels — ' His voice was almost sorry: 'When a woman gets an idea in her head.'

'Of course.'

'It's going to be all right. I think she sees now that you can provide for the child, and so we can't very well stand in your way or Honoria's way.'

'Thank you, Lincoln.'

'I'd better go along and see how she is.'

'I'm going.'

He was still trembling when he reached the street, but as he crossed the River Seine, he felt fresh and new and happy. But back in his room he couldn't sleep. His thoughts of Helen troubled him. Helen whom he had loved so until they had begun to hurt each other senselessly. On that terrible February night that Marion remembered so clearly, a slow quarrel had gone on for hours. Then they made a scene* in the restaurant. When he arrived home alone he turned the key in the lock in wild anger. How could he know she would arrive an hour later alone, that there would be a snowstorm in which she wandered about in slippers, too confused to find a taxi? Afterwards, she got very sick and

*made a scene, displayed one's temper in public.

61

nearly died. Marion thought it to be one of the many scenes her sister suffered and she never forgot.

Going over it again brought Helen nearer, and in the white, soft light that steals upon half sleep near morning he found himself talking to her again. She said that he was perfectly right about Honoria and that she wanted Honoria to be with him. She said she was glad he was being good and doing better. She said a lot of other things – very friendly things – but she was on a swing in a white dress, and swinging faster and faster all the time, so that at the end he could not hear clearly all that she said.

An unfortunate incident

He woke up feeling happy. The door of the world was open again. He made plans, for Honoria and himself, but suddenly he grew sad, remembering all the plans he and Helen had made. She had not planned to die. The present was the thing – work to do and someone to love.

It was another bright, clear day. He called Lincoln Peters at the bank where he worked and asked if he could take Honoria when he left for Prague. Lincoln agreed that there was no reason for delay. One thing, the legal guardianship, Marion wanted to keep a while longer. She was upset by the whole matter, and it would be easier for her if she felt that the situation was still in her control for another year. Charlie agreed, wanting only the child he could see and touch.

He lunched with Lincoln Peters, trying not to appear too happy.

'There's nothing quite like your own child,' Lincoln said. 'But you understand how Marion feels too.'

'She's forgotten how hard I worked for seven years,' Charlie said. 'She just remembers one night.'

'There's another thing.' Lincoln hesitated. 'While you and Helen were going around Europe throwing money away, we were just making ends meet*. I think Marion felt there was some kind of injustice in it — you not even working towards the end, and getting richer and richer.'

'It went just as quickly as it came,' said Charlie.

'Yes, — well, the big party's over now. I just said that   *5* to explain Marion's feelings about those crazy years. If you drop in about six o'clock tonight before Marion's too tired, we'll settle the details on the spot.'

At five he took a taxi and bought presents for all the Peters — a cloth doll, a box of Roman soldiers, flowers   *10* for Marion, handkerchiefs for Lincoln.

He saw, when he arrived in the apartment, that Marion had accepted the inevitable. Honoria had been told she was going; she tried not to show too much of her happiness in front of the others. Only on his lap did she whisper her   *15* delight and the question "when?" before she slipped away with the other children.

He and Marion were alone for a minute in the room, and on an impulse he spoke out boldly:

'Family quarrels are bitter things. They don't go according   *20* to any rules. They don't heal easily. I wish you and I could be on better terms.'

'Some things are hard to forget,' she answered. 'It's a question of confidence.' There was no answer to this and presently she asked, 'When do you propose to take her?'   *25*

'As soon as I can get someone to look after her. I hope the day after tomorrow.'

'That's impossible. I've got to get her things in shape. Not before Saturday.'

He yielded. Coming back into the room, Lincoln offered   *30* him a drink.

The doorbell rang. The maid went down the corridor to answer it. When she came back, she was closely followed by voices, which turned out to be those of Duncan Schaeffer and Lorraine Quarrles.   *35*

They were roaring with laughter and they were drunk. For

*making ends meet, balancing one's income with one's expenditure.

a moment Charlie was taken by surprise; unable to understand how they had found out the Peters' address.

Anxious and at a loss, Charlie shook hands with them quickly and introduced them to Lincoln and Marion. Marion just nodded. She had drawn back a step towards the fire, *5* her little girl stood beside her, and Marion put an arm about her shoulder.

With growing annoyance at the unwelcome visit, Charlie waited for them to explain themselves. Duncan said:

'We came to invite you out to dinner. Lorraine and I *10* insist that all this secret business about your address has got to stop.'

Charlie came closer to them, as if to force them backwards down the corridor.

'Sorry, but I can't. Tell me where you'll be and I'll phone *15* you in half an hour.'

'Come on. I'm sure your cousins won't mind. See you so seldom.'

'I can't,' said Charlie sharply. 'You two have dinner and I'll phone you.' *20*

Her voice became suddenly unpleasant. 'All right, we'll go. But I remember once when you hammered on my door at four a.m. I was enough of a good sport to give you a drink. Come on, Dunc.'

With angry faces, and uncertain feet, they got up and *25* left.

'Good night,' Charlie said.

'Good night!' Lorraine answered.

When he went back into the room Marion had not moved, only now her son was standing in the circle of her other *30* arm. Lincoln was still swinging Honoria back and forth.

'What an outrage!' Charlie broke out.

Neither of them answered.

'People I haven't seen for two years having the nerve* . . .'

He broke off. Marion had made the sound 'Oh!' in one *35*

having the nerve, an expression which suggests disapproval of a certain behaviour.

65

short, angry breath, turned her body from him with a sudden movement and left the room.

Lincoln set down Honoria carefully.

'You children go in and start your soup,' he said, and when
5 they obeyed, he said to Charlie:

'Marion's not well and she can't stand shocks. Those kind of people make her really physically sick.'

'I didn't tell them to come here. They somehow got your name from somebody. They — '

10 'Well, it's too bad. It doesn't help matters. Excuse me a minute.'

Left alone, Charlie waited uneasily in his chair. In the next room he could hear the children eating, talking, unaffected by what had just happened.

15 In a minute Lincoln came back. 'Look here, Charlie. I think we'd better call off dinner for tonight. Marion's not feeling well.'

'Is she angry with me?'

'Sort of,' he said, almost roughly. 'She's not strong and — '
20 'You mean she's changed her mind about Honoria?'

'She's pretty bitter right now. I don't know. You phone me at the bank tomorrow.'

'I wish you'd explain to her I never dreamed those people would come here. I'm just as unhappy as you are.'

25 'I couldn't explain anything to her now.'

Charlie got up. He took his coat and hat and started down the corridor. Then he opened the door of the dining-room and said in a strange voice, 'Good night, children.'

Honoria rose and ran around the table to hug him.

Wait for six months

30 Charlie went directly to the Ritz bar to look for Lorraine and Duncan, but they were not there, and he realized that in any case there was nothing he could do. He had not touched his drink at the Peters', and now he ordered one.

The bartender came over to say hello.

'It's a great change,' he said sadly. 'We do about half the business we did. So many fellows I hear about back in the States lost every cent, I hear. Are you back in the States?' 5

'No, I'm in business in Prague.'

'I heard that you lost a lot in the crash.'

'I did,' and he added grimly, 'but I lost everything I wanted in the boom*.'

Again the memory of those days swept over him like 10 a nightmare — the men who locked their wives out in the snow, because the snow of 1929 wasn't real snow. If you didn't want it to be snow, you just paid some money.

He went to the phone and called the Peters' apartment; Lincoln answered. 15

'I called up because this thing is on my mind. Has Marion said anything definite?'

'Marion's sick,' Lincoln answered impatiently. 'I know this thing isn't altogether your fault, but I can't have her go to pieces about it. I'm afraid we'll have to forget the 20 matter for six months.'

'I see.'

'I'm sorry, Charlie.'

He went back to his table lost in thoughts. There wasn't much he could do now except send Honoria some things; 25 he would send her a lot of things tomorrow. He thought rather angrily that this was just money — he had given so many people money . . . .

He would come back some day; they couldn't make him pay forever. But he wanted his child, and nothing else 30 was much good now. He wasn't young any more, with a lot of nice thoughts and dreams to have by himself. He was absolutely sure Helen wouldn't have wanted him to be so alone.

*boom, sudden increase in trade activity.

4

Gretchen's Forty Winks

====

The plan

The sidewalks were covered with brittle leaves. It was sure
to snow before dark. Autumn was over. Soon it would be
Christmas. Roger Halsey, standing at his own house, decided
that he hadn't time for worrying about the weather. Then
5 he let himself hurriedly into the house, and shut the subject
out into the cold twilight.

The hall was dark, but from above he heard the voices
of his wife and the nursemaid and the baby in one of their
endless conversations.

10 Roger turned on the hall light and walked into the living-
room and turned on the red silk lamp. He put his thick
portfolio* on the table and sitting down, rested his intense
young face in his hands for a few minutes, shading his eyes
carefully from the light. Then he lit a cigarette, squashed
15 it out, and going to the foot of the stairs called for his wife.

'Gretchen!'

'Hello, dear!' Her voice was full of laughter. 'Come see
baby.'

'I can't see baby now,' he said aloud. 'How long before
20 you'll be down?'

'Oh, I'll be right down.'

'How soon?' he shouted.

Tonight he was deliberately impatient. It almost disappointed him when Gretchen came running down the
25 stairs, three at a time, crying, 'What is it?' in a rather surprised
voice.

They kissed. They had been married three years, and
they were very much in love.

'Come in here,' he said abruptly. 'I want to talk to you.'

*portfolio, a case for carrying papers etc.

His wife, a red-head, followed him into the living-room.

'Listen, Gretchen', he sat down at the end of the sofa, 'beginning with tonight I'm going to — what's the matter?'

'Nothing. I'm just looking for a cigarette. Go on.'

She tiptoed back to the sofa and settled at the other end. 5

'Gretchen — ' Again he broke off. 'Well, what is it?' he asked wildly.

'Matches.'

'What?'

'Thank you,' she whispered, when he impatiently handed 10 her a box of matches. 'I didn't mean to interrupt you. Go on.'

When he was in this mood her slightest action irritated him beyond measure.

'When you've got time to listen,' he said crossly, 'you 15 might be interested in discussing something terrible!'

'Terrible?'

Her eyes were wide, startled; she sat quiet as a mouse.

'That was just to get your attention. But, beginning tonight, I start on what'll probably be the most important 20 six weeks that'll decide whether we're going on forever in this rotten little house in this rotten little town.'

At this point Gretchen seemed to lose interest in the conversation. She was a Southern girl, and any question that had to do with getting ahead in the world always tended 25 to give her a headache.

'Six months ago I left the New York Lithographic Company,' announced Roger, 'and went into the advertising business for myself.'

'I know,' interrupted Gretchen with displeasure, 'and 30 now instead of getting six hundred a month, we're living on five hundred.'

'Gretchen,' said Roger sharply, 'if you'll just believe in me as hard as you can for six weeks more we'll be rich. I've got a chance now to get some of the biggest accounts 35 in the country.' He hesitated. 'And for these six weeks we won't go out at all, and we won't have anyone here. I'm going to bring home work every night, and we'll pull down all the blinds and if anyone rings the doorbell we won't answer.'

He smiled as if it were a new game they were going to
5 play. Then, as Gretchen was silent, his smile faded, and he looked at her uncertainly.

'Well, what's the matter?' she broke out finally. 'Do you expect me to jump up and sing? You do enough work as it is. If you try to do any more you'll end up having a
10 nervous breakdown. I read about a — '

'Don't worry about me,' he interrupted, 'I'm all right. But you're going to be bored to death sitting here every evening.'

'No, I won't,' she said, ' — except tonight.'
15 'What about tonight?'

'George Tompkins asked us to dinner.'

'Did you accept?'

'Of course I did,' she said impatiently. 'Why not? You're always talking about what a terrible neighbourhood this is,
20 and I thought maybe you'd like to go to a nicer one for a change.'

'When I go to a nicer neighbourhood I want to go for good,' he said grimly.

'Well, can we go?'
25 'I suppose we'll have to if you've accepted.'

Dinner at George's

The conversation abruptly ended. Gretchen jumped up and kissed him and rushed into the kitchen to light the hot water for a bath. With a sigh he carefully put his port-folio behind the bookcase — it contained only drawings
30 for display advertising, but it seemed to him the first thing a burglar would look for. Then he went upstairs, and began dressing for dinner.

They had no car, so George Tompkins called for them

at 6.30. Tompkins was a successful interior decorator, a broad, rosy man with a handsome moustache. He and Roger had once been close friends in New York, but they had met only a few times in the past five years.

'We ought to see each other more,' he told Roger to- 5
night. 'You ought to go out more often, old boy. Cocktail?'

'No, thanks.'

'No? Well, your fair wife will — won't you, Gretchen?'

'I love this house,' she exclaimed, taking the glass and looking admiringly at the fashionable decorations in the 10
room.

'I like it,' said Tompkins with satisfaction. 'I did it to please myself, and I succeeded.'

Roger started moodily around the stiff, plain room, wondering if they could have wandered into the kitchen 15
by mistake.

'You look like the devil, Roger,' said his host. 'Have a cocktail and cheer up.'

'Have one,' urged Gretchen.

'What?' Roger turned around absently. 'Oh, no, thanks. 20
I've got to work after I get home.'

'Work!' Tompkins smiled. 'Listen, Roger, you'll kill yourself with work. Why don't you bring a little balance into your life — work a little, then play a little?'

'That's what I tell him,' said Gretchen. 25

'Do you know an average business man's day?' demanded Tompkins as they went in to dinner. 'Coffee in the morning, eight hours' work interrupted by a quick lunch, and then home again with indigestion and a bad temper to give the wife a pleasant evening.' 30

Roger laughed shortly.

'You've been going to the movies too much,' he said dryly.

'What?' Tompkins looked at him with some irritation. 'Movies? I've hardly ever been to the movies in my life. I think the movies are terrible. My opinion on life is drawn 35
from my own observations. I believe in a balanced life.'

'What's that?' demanded Roger.

71

'Well — ' he hesitated, ' — probably the best way to tell you would be to describe my own day. Would that seem horribly egotistic*?'

'Oh, no!' Gretchen looked at him with interest. 'I'd love
5 to hear about it.'

'Well, in the morning I get up and go through a series of exercises. I've got one room fitted up as a little gymnasium, and I punch the bag and do shadow-boxing and weight-pulling for an hour. Then after a cold bath — there's a thing
10 now! Do you take a daily cold bath?'

'No,' admitted Roger, 'I take a hot bath in the evening three or four times a week.'

A horrified silence fell. Tompkins and Gretchen exchanged a glance as if something improper had been said.

15 'What's the matter?' broke out Roger, glancing from one to the other with some irritation. 'You know I don't take a bath every day — I haven't got the time.'

Tompkins gave a prolonged sigh.

'After my bath,' he continued, 'I have breakfast and
20 drive to my office in New York, where I work until four. Then I lay off, and if it's summer I hurry out here for nine holes of golf, or if it's winter I play squash for an hour at my club. Then a good game of bridge until dinner.'

'Dinner may have something to do with business, but
25 in a pleasant way. Perhaps I've just finished a house for some customer, and he wants me to be on hand for his first party to see that the lighting is soft enough and all that sort of thing. Or maybe I sit down with a good book of poetry and spend the evening alone. At any rate, I do
30 something every night to get me out of myself.'

'It must be wonderful,' said Gretchen enthusiastically. 'I wish we lived like that.'

Tompkins bent forward earnestly over the table.

'You can,' he said impressively. 'There's no reason why
35 you shouldn't. Look here, if Roger'll play nine holes of golf every day it'll do wonders for him. He won't know

egotistic, conceited, selfish.

72

himself. He'll do his work better, never get that tired, nervous feeling — what's the matter?'

He broke off. Roger had yawned.

'Roger,' cried Gretchen sharply, 'there's no need to be so rude. If you did what George said, you'd be a lot better off.' She turned indignantly to their host. 'The latest is that he's going to work at night for the next six weeks. He says he's going to pull down the blinds and shut us up like hermits in a cave. He's going to do it every night for six weeks.'

Tompkins shook his head sadly.

'At the end of six weeks,' he remarked, 'he'll find himself in a hospital bed. Let me tell you, every private hospital in New York is full of cases like yours. You just strain the human nervous system a little too far, and bang! — you're laid up sixty weeks for repairs.' He broke off, changed his tone, and turned to Gretchen with a smile, 'Not to mention what happens to you. It seems to me it's the wife rather than the husband who suffers most under these circumstances.'

'I don't mind,' protested Gretchen loyally.

'Yes, she does,' said Roger grimly, 'she minds like the devil. She's a shortsighted little egg, and she thinks it's going to be forever until I get started and she can have some new clothes. But it can't be helped.'

'Your ideas on women are about twenty years out of date,' said Tompkins pityingly.

'If a girl marries a young man for love,' insisted Roger, 'she ought to be willing to make any sacrifice within reason, so long as her husband keeps going ahead.'

'Let's not talk about it,' said Gretchen impatiently. 'Please, Roger, let's have a good time just this once.'

Roger said nothing.

Roger starts his work

When Tompkins dropped them in front of their house at eleven Roger and Gretchen stood for a moment on the sidewalk looking at the winter moon. There was a fine, damp, dusty snow in the air, and Roger drew a long breath
5 of it and put his arm around Gretchen.

'I can make more money than he can,' he said tensely. 'And I'll be doing it in just forty days.'

'Forty days,' she sighed. 'It seems such a long time — when everybody else is always having fun. If I could only
10 sleep for forty days.'

'Why don't you, honey? Just take forty winks, and when you wake up everything'll be fine.'

She was silent for a moment.

'Roger,' she asked thoughtfully, 'do you think George
15 meant what he said about taking me horseback riding on Sunday?'

Roger frowned.

'I don't know. Probably not — I hope he didn't.' He hesitated. 'As a matter of fact, he made me sort of sore
20 tonight — all that rubbish about his cold bath.'

With their arms about each other, they started up the walk to the house.

'I'll bet he doesn't take a cold bath every morning,' continued Roger, 'or three times a week, either.' He fumbled
25 in his pocket for the key and put it in the lock sharply. 'I'll bet he hasn't had a bath for a month.'

A fortnight on

After a fortnight of intensive work, Roger Halsey's days passed by in blocks of twos and threes and fours. From eight until 5.30 he was in his office. Then a half-hour on the
30 train, where he scrawled notes on the backs of envelopes under the dull yellow light. By 7.30 his crayons, scissors,

and sheets of white cardboard were spread over the living-room table, and he worked there with much grunting and sighing until midnight, while Gretchen lay on the sofa with a book. At twelve there was always an argument as to whether he would come to bed. He would agree to come *5* after he had cleared up everything. When he finally did, he usually found Gretchen sound asleep.

Sometimes it was three o'clock before Roger finished his work, and he would undress in the dark, his body almost coming apart, but with a sense of triumph that he had *10* lasted out another day.

Christmas came and went and he scarcely noticed that it was gone. He remembered it afterwards as the day he completed the art-work for Garrod's Shoes. This was one of the eight large accounts for which he was aiming in *15* January — if he got half of them he was assured a quarter of a million dollars' worth of business during the year.

But the world outside his business became a disorderly dream. He was aware that on two cool December Sundays George Tompkins had taken Gretchen horseback riding, *20* and that another time she had gone out with him in his car to spend the afternoon skiing on the country-club hill. A picture of Tompkins, in an expensive frame, had appeared one morning on their bedroom wall. And one night he was shocked into a protest when Gretchen went to the *25* theatre with Tompkins in town.

But his work was almost done. Daily now his layouts arrived from the printers until seven of them were piled in his office safe. He knew how good they were. Money alone couldn't buy such work; more than he realized himself, *30* it had been a labour of love.

December fell like a dead leaf from the calendar. There was a painful week when he had to give up coffee because it made his heart pound so. If he could hold on now for four days — three days — *35*

On Thursday afternoon H. G. Garrod was to arrive in New York. On Wednesday evening Roger came home at

seven to find Gretchen poring over the December bills with a strange expression in her eyes.

'What's the matter?'

She nodded at the bills. He ran through them frowning.

5   'Gosh!'

'I can't help it,' she burst out suddenly. 'They're terrible.'

'Well, I didn't marry you because you were a wonderful housekeeper. I'll manage about the bills some way. Don't worry your little head over it.'

10   She regarded him coldly.

'You talk as if I were a child.'

'I have to,' he said with sudden irritation.

'Well, at least I'm not a piece of something that you can just put somewhere and forget.'

15   He knelt down by her quickly, and took her arms in his hands.

'Gretchen, listen!' he said breathlessly. 'For God's sake, don't go to pieces now! This is no time for a quarrel. If

76

we quarrel, we'll only hurt ourselves. I love you, Gretchen. Say you love me — quick!'

'You know I love you.'

The quarrel was for a moment forgotten. After dinner when he began to spread his working materials on the table, *5* Gretchen was obviously displeased.

'Oh, Roger,' she protested, 'I thought you didn't have to work tonight.'

'I didn't think I'd have to, but something came up.'

'I've invited George Tompkins over.' *10*

'Oh, gosh!' he exclaimed. 'Well, I'm sorry, honey, but you'll have to phone him not to come.'

'He's left,' she said. 'He's coming straight from town. He'll be here any minute now.'

Roger groaned. He thought of sending them both to the *15* movies, but somehow he did not suggest it. He did not really want her at the movies; he wanted her here, where he could look up and know she was by his side.

George arrives

George Tompkins arrived at eight o'clock. 'Aha!' he cried reprovingly, coming into the room. 'Still at it.'

Roger agreed coolly that he was.

'Better quit — better quit before you have to.' He sat
5 down with a long sigh of physical comfort and lit a cigarette. 'Take it from a fellow who's looked into the question scientifically. We can stand so much, and then — bang!'

'If you'll excuse me,' Roger made his voice as polite as possible, 'I'm going upstairs to finish this work.'

10 'Just as you like, Roger,' George waved his hand carelessly. 'It isn't that I mind. I'm the friend of the family and I'd just as soon see the missus as the mister.' He smiled playfully. 'But if I were you, old boy, I'd put away my work and get a good night's sleep.'

15 When Roger had spread out his materials on the bed upstairs he found that he could still hear the murmur of their voices through the thin floor. He began wondering what they found to talk about. The thought began to bother him as he worked, and several times he arose and paced ner-
20 vously up and down the room.

The bed was not a suitable place for work. Several times the paper slipped from the board on which it rested, and the pencil punched through. Everything was wrong tonight.

At ten he realized that he had done nothing for more
25 than an hour, and with a sudden exclamation he gathered together his papers, put them in his portfolio, and went downstairs. They were sitting together on the sofa when he came in.

'Oh, hello!' cried Gretchen, rather unnecessarily, he
30 thought. 'We were just discussing you.'

'Thank you,' he answered ironically. 'Which part of my body were you examining?'

'Your health,' said Tompkins jovially.

'My health's all right,' answered Roger shortly.

35 'But you look at it so selfishly, old fella,' cried Tompkins.

'You only consider yourself in the matter. Don't you think Gretchen has any rights? If you were working on a wonderful work of art — why, then I'd say go ahead. But you're not. It's just some silly advertisement about how to sell some hair tonic, and if all the hair tonic ever made was dumped into   5 the ocean tomorrow the world wouldn't be one bit the worse for it.'

'Wait a minute,' said Roger angrily, 'that's not quite fair. I'm not fooling myself about the importance of my work — it's just as useless as the stuff you do. But to   10 Gertchen and me it's just about the most important thing in the world.'

'Are you implying that my work is useless?' demanded Tompkins.

'No, not if it brings happiness to some poor fool who   15 doesn't know how to spend his money.'

Tompkins and Gretchen exchanged a glance.

'Oh-h-h!' exclaimed Tompkins ironically. 'I didn't realize that all these years I've just been wasting my time.'

'You're an idler,' said Roger rudely.   20

'Me?' cried Tompkins angrily. 'You call me an idler because I have a little balance in my life and find time to do interesting things? Because I play hard as well as work hard and don't let myself get to be dull and tiresome.'

Both men were angry now, and their voices had risen,   25 though on Tompkins' face there still remained the semblance of a smile.

'What I object to,' said Roger steadily, 'is that for the last six weeks you seem to have done all your playing around here.'   30

'Roger!' cried Gretchen. 'What do you mean by talking like that?'

'Just what I said.'

'You've just lost your temper.' Tompkins lit a cigarette, appearing to be calm. 'You're so nervous from overwork   35 you don't know what you're saying. You're about to have a nervous break — '

'You get out of here!' cried Roger fiercely. 'You get out of here right now — before I throw you out!'

'You — you throw me out?' he cried incredulously.

They were actually moving towards each other when Gretchen stepped between them. Grabbing Tompkins' arm, she urged him towards the door.

'He's acting like a fool, George, but you'd better get out,' she cried.

'He insulted me!' shouted Tompkins. 'He threatened to throw me out!'

'Never mind, George,' pleaded Gretchen. 'He doesn't know what he's saying. Please go! I'll see you at ten o'clock tomorrow.'

She opened the door.

'You won't see him at ten o'clock tomorrow,' said Roger steadily. 'He's not coming to this house any more.'

Tompkins turned to Gretchen.

'It's his house,' he suggested. 'Perhaps we'd better meet at mine.'

Then he was gone, and Gretchen had shut the door behind him. Her eyes were full of angry tears.

'See what you've done!' she sobbed. 'The only friend I had. The only person in the world who liked me enough to treat me decently, is insulted by my husband in my own house.'

She threw herself on the sofa and began to cry passionately into the cushions.

'He brought it on himself,' said Roger stubbornly. 'I've stood as much as my self-respect will allow. I don't want you going out with him any more.'

'I *will* go out with him!' cried Gretchen wildly. 'I'll go out with him all I want! Do you think it's any fun living here with you?'

'Gretchen,' he said coldly, 'get up and put on your hat and coat and go out of that door and never come back!'

'But I don't want to go out,' she said in confusion.

'Well, then behave yourself.' And he added in a gentler

voice, 'I thought you were going to sleep for these forty days.'
'Oh, yes,' she cried bitterly, 'easy enough to say! But I'm
tired of sleeping.' She got up and faced him defiantly. 'And
what's more, I'm going riding with George Tompkins tomorrow.'   5
'You won't go out with him if I have to take you to New
York and sit you down in my office until I get through.'
She looked at him with wild anger in her eyes.
'I hate you,' she said slowly. 'And I'd like to take all
the work you've done and tear it up and throw it in the   10
fire. And just to give you something to worry about tomorrow, I probably won't be here when you get back.'
She got up from the sofa, and looked at her flushed,
tear-stained face in the mirror. Then she ran upstairs and
shut herself into the bedroom.   15

Roger continues his work

Automatically Roger spread out his work on the living-
room table. Very soon he was deep in work. He could hear
no sound but the scratch of his crayon on paper. His eyes
took in nothing but the bright colours of the designs.
After a long while he looked at his watch — it was after   20
three. The wind had come up outside and was rushing by
the house corners making a sound, like a heavy body falling
through space. He stopped his work and listened. He was
not tired now but his head felt like a bundle of raw nerves.
Suddenly he began to be afraid. A hundred warnings   25
he had heard swept into his mind. People did break themselves with overwork, and his body and brain were made
of the same stuff. For the first time he found himself envying
George Tompkins' calm nerves and healthy routine. He
arose and began pacing the room in a panic.   30
'I've got to sleep,' he whispered to himself tensely. 'Other-
wise I'll go crazy.'
He rubbed his hand over his eyes, and returned to the

table to put up his work, but his fingers were shaking so that he could scarcely hold the board. The sway of a bare branch against the window made him start and cry out. He sat down on the sofa and tried to think.

5 'Stop! Stop! Stop!' the clock said. 'Stop! Stop! Stop!'
'I can't stop,' he answered aloud. 'I can't afford to stop.'

Dragging his limbs wearily into the kitchen, he brought the alarm-clock into the living-room and set it for seven. Then he wrapped himself in his overcoat, lay down on
10 the sofa and fell immediately into a heavy, dreamless sleep.

When he awoke the light was still shining weakly, but the room was the grey colour of a winter morning. He got up, and looking anxiously at his hands, found to his relief that they no longer trembled. He felt much better.
15 Then he began to remember in detail the events of the night before, and his worries started afresh. There was work ahead of him, twenty-four hours of work, and Gretchen, whether she wanted to or not, must sleep for one more day.

20 Roger's mind lit up suddenly as if he had just thought of a new advertising idea. A few minutes later he was hurrying through the sharp morning air to Kingsley's drug-store.

Breakfast for Gretchen

At 7.30 back home again, Roger walked into his own kitchen. The general housework girl had just arrived and
25 was taking off her hat.

'I want you to cook Mrs Halsey's breakfast right away. I'll take it up myself.'

When that was done, he secretly put into the coffee half a teaspoonful of a white substance that was not
30 powdered sugar. Then he mounted the stairs and opened the door of the bedroom.

Gretchen woke up with a start. She was first astonished

to find Roger in the room. Then when she saw the breakfast in his hand, her astonishment changed to contempt. She thought he was trying to make peace.

'I don't want any breakfast,' she said coldly, and his heart sank, 'except some coffee.'

'No breakfast?' Roger's voice expressed disappointment.

'I said I'd take some coffee.'

Roger left the tray on a table beside the bed and returned quickly to the kitchen.

'We're going away until tomorrow afternoon,' he told the maid, 'and I want to close up the house right now. So you just put on your hat and go home.'

He looked at his watch. It was ten minutes to eight, and he wanted to catch the 8.10 train. He waited five minutes and then tiptoed softly upstairs and into Gretchen's room. She was sound asleep. The coffee cup was empty. He looked at her rather anxiously, but her breathing was regular and clear.

From the closet he took a suitcase and very quickly began filling it with her shoes. He had not realized that she owned so many pairs. When he closed the suitcase it was bulging.

He hesitated a minute, took a pair of scissors from a box, and following the telephone-wire until it went out of sight behind the dresser, cut it. He jumped as there was a soft knock at the door. It was the nursemaid. He had forgotten her.

'Mrs Halsey and I are going up to the city till tomorrow,' he lied. 'Take the baby to the beach and have lunch there. Stay all day.'

Back in the room, a wave of pity passed over him. Gretchen seemed suddenly lovely and helpless, sleeping there. It was somehow terrible to rob her young life of a day. He touched her hair with his fingers, and as she murmured something in her dreams he leaned over and kissed her bright cheek. Then he picked up the suitcase full of shoes, locked the door, and ran down the stairs.

Waiting

By five o'clock that afternoon the last package of cards for Garrod's shoes had been sent by messenger to H. G. Garrod at the Biltmore Hotel. He was to give a decision the next morning. At 5.30 Roger's secretary tapped him on
5 the shoulder.

'Mr Golden, the superintendent of the building, to see you.'

Roger turned around dazedly.

'Oh, how do?'

10 Mr Golden came directly to the point. If Mr Halsey intended to keep the office any longer, he would have to pay up the rent he owed.

'Mr Golden,' said Roger wearily, 'everything'll be all right tomorrow. If you worry me now maybe you'll never
15 get your money. After tomorrow nothing will matter.'

Mr Golden looked at him uneasily. Young men did foolish things with themselves when business went wrong. Then his eyes fell unpleasantly on the suitcase beside the desk.

'Going on a trip?' he asked.

20 'What? Oh, no. That's just some clothes.'

'Clothes, eh? Well, Mr Halsey, just to prove that you mean what you say, suppose you let me keep that suitcase until tomorrow noon.'

'Just a matter of form,' he remarked.

25 'I understand,' said Roger, swinging around to his desk. 'Good afternoon.'

Mr Golden seemed to feel that the conversation should close on a softer note.

'And don't work too hard, Mr Halsey. You don't want
30 to have a nervous break — '

'No,' shouted Roger, 'I don't. But I will if you don't leave me alone.'

As the door closed behind Mr Golden, Roger's secretary turned around sympathetically.

35 'You shouldn't have let him get away with that,' she said.

'What's in there? Clothes?'

'No,' answered Roger absently. 'Just all my wife's shoes.'

He slept in the office that night on a sofa beside his desk. At dawn he awoke with a nervous start, rushed out into the street for coffee, and returned in ten minutes in a panic — afraid that he might have missed Mr Garrod's telephone call. It was then 6.30.

By eight o'clock his whole body seemed to be on fire. When his two artists arrived he was stretched on the couch in almost physical pain. The phone rang loudly at 9.30, and he picked up the receiver with trembling hands.

'Hello.'

'Is this the Halsey agency?'

'Yes, this is Mr Halsey speaking.'

'This is Mr H. G. Garrod.'

Roger's heart stopped beating.

'I called up, young fellow, to say that this is wonderful work you've given us here. We want all of it and as much more as your office can do.'

'Oh, God!' cried Roger.

'What?' Mr H. G. Garrod was considerably startled. 'Say, wait a minute there!'

But he was talking to nobody. The phone dropped to the floor, and Roger, stretched full length on the couch, was sobbing as if his heart would break.

Gretchen loses a day

Three hours later, his face somewhat pale, but his eyes calm as a child's, Roger opened the door of his wife's bedroom with the morning paper under his arm. At the sound of his footsteps she woke up.

'What time is it?' she demanded.

He looked at his watch.

Suddenly she began to cry.

'Roger,' she said brokenly, 'I'm sorry about last night.'

85

He nodded coolly.

'Everything's all right now,' he answered. Then, after a pause: 'I've got the account — the biggest one.'

She turned towards him quickly.

5 'You have?' Then, after a minute's silence: 'Can I have a new dress?'

'Dress?' He laughed shortly. 'You can have a dozen. This account alone will bring us in forty thousand a year. It's one of the biggest in the West.'

10 She looked at him, startled.

'Forty thousand a year!'

'Yes.'

'Gosh' — and then faintly — 'I didn't know it'd really be anything like that.' Again she thought a minute, 'We

15 can have a house like George Tompkins'.'

'I don't want an interior-decoration shop.'

'Forty thousand a year!' she repeated again, and then added softly: 'Oh, Roger — '

'Yes?'

20 'I'm not going out with George Tompkins.'

'I wouldn't let you, even if you wanted to,' he said shortly.

She made a show of indignation.

'Why, I've had a date with him for this Thursday for weeks.'

25 'It isn't Thursday.'

'It is.'

'It's Friday.'

'Why, Roger, you must be crazy! Don't you think I know what day it is?'

30 'It isn't Thursday,' he said stubbornly. 'Look!' And he held out the morning paper.

'Friday!' she exclaimed. 'Why, this is a mistake! This must be last week's paper. Today's Thursday.'

She closed her eyes and thought for a moment.

35 'Yesterday was Wednesday,' she said decisively. 'The laundress came yesterday. I guess I know.'

'Well, look at the paper. There isn't any question about it.'

86

With a bewildered look on her face she got out of bed and began searching for her clothes. Roger went into the bathroom to shave. A minute later he heard Gretchen getting back into bed.

'What's the matter?' he inquired, putting his head around the corner of the bathroom. 5

'I'm scared,' she said in a trembling voice. 'I think my nerves are giving away. I can't find any of my shoes.'

'Your shoes? Why, the closet's full of them.'

'I know, but I can't see one.' Her face was pale with fear. 'Oh, Roger.' 10

'I'll get the doctor,' he said.

He walked remorselessly to the telephone and took up the receiver.

'Phone seems to be out of order,' he remarked after a minute, 'I'll send the maid.' 15

The doctor arrived in ten minutes.

'I think I'm going to collapse,' Gretchen told him in a strained voice.

Doctor Gregory sat down on the edge of the bed and took her wrist in his hand. 20

'I got up,' said Gretchen in a frightened voice, 'and I found that I'd lost a whole day. I had an engagement to go riding with George Tompkins — '

'What?' exclaimed the doctor in surprise. Then he laughed. 25

'George Tompkins won't go riding with anyone for many days to come.'

'Has he gone away?' asked Gretchen curiously.

'He's going West.'

'Why?' demanded Roger. 'Is he running away with some- 30
body's wife?

'No,' said Doctor Gregory. 'He's had a nervous break-down.'

'What?' they exclaimed in unison.

'He just collapsed in his cold shower.' 35

'But he was always talking about his — his balanced life,' gasped Gretchen. 'He had it on his mind.'

'I know,' said the doctor. 'He's been talking about it all morning. I think it's driven him a little mad. He worked pretty hard at it, you know.'

'At what?' demanded Roger in bewilderment.

5 'At keeping his life balanced.' He turned to Gretchen. 'Now all I'll prescribe for this lady here is a good rest. If she'll just stay around the house for a few days and take forty winks of sleep she'll be as fit as ever. She's been under some strain.'

10 'Doctor,' exclaimed Roger, 'don't you think I'd better have a rest or something? I've been working pretty hard lately.'

'You!' Doctor Gregory laughed, slapping him hard on the back. 'My boy, I never saw you looking better in your 15 life.'

Roger turned away quickly to hide his smile and winked forty times, or almost forty times, at the picture of Mr George Tompkins, which hung slightly askew on the bedroom wall.

Questions

1
The Diamond as big as the Ritz

A. Describe John T. Unger's background.
B. How did John spend his summers when attending St Midas's School?
C. Describe the journey from school to Percy's home.
D. Imagine you are Percy. In your own words, tell John the story of the Washington family.
E. With your partner have the conversation you think John and Kismine had at their first meeting.
F. What did John think would happen to him when the holiday came to an end?
G. Describe the events on the night of "The Battle".

2
Basil: The Freshest Boy

A. Where was Basil Lee going and who was his companion?
B. Why did Basil want to go to New York?
C. Pretend you and your partner are Basil and Fat Gasper and act out their conversation.
D. What did Treadway do?
E. Outline what Basil did when Mr Rooney left him on his own in New York.
F. Describe the events leading up to "Basil's Decision".

3
Babylon Revisited

A. Why was Charlie in Paris?

B. Who was Marion and what was her attitude towards Charlie?
C. Outline what Honoria and Charlie did after lunch.
D. Who were Lorraine and Duncan and where did they bump into Charlie?
E. In groups of three (you are Marion, Charlie and Lincoln) act out the conversation they had about Honoria.
F. In Marion's opinion what events led up to Helen's death?
G. How did Lorraine and Duncan's visit spoil things for Charlie?
H. What was the outcome of their visit?

4
Gretchen's Forty Winks

A. What important plan did Roger have to tell Gretchen about?
B. Who was George Tompkins?
C. Describe a typical day in the life of George Tompkins.
D. Why did Roger go to Kinsley's Drug-store?
E. Describe exactly what Roger did after taking Gretchen her breakfast.
F. Did Roger get the account for Garrod Shoes?
G. What happened to George Tompkins and why was it so ironic?

Oxford Progressive English Readers

Introductory Grade

Vocabulary restricted to 1400 headwords
Illustrated in full colour

The Call of the Wild and Other Stories	Jack London
Emma	Jane Austen
Jungle Book Stories	Rudyard Kipling
Life Without Katy and Seven Other Stories	O. Henry
Little Women	Louisa M. Alcott
The Lost Umbrella of Kim Chu	Eleanor Estes
Stories from Vanity Fair	W.M. Thackeray
Tales from the Arabian Nights	Retold by Rosemary Border
Treasure Island	R.L. Stevenson

Grade 1

Vocabulary restricted to 2100 headwords
Illustrated in full colour

The Adventures of Sherlock Holmes	Sir Arthur Conan Doyle
Alice's Adventures in Wonderland	Lewis Carroll
A Christmas Carol	Charles Dickens
The Dagger and Wings and Other Father Brown Stories	G.K. Chesterton
The Flying Heads and Other Strange Stories	Retold by C. Nancarrow
The Golden Touch and Other Stories	Retold by R. Border
Great Expectations	Charles Dickens
Gulliver's Travels	Jonathan Swift
Hijacked!	J.M. Marks
Jane Eyre	Charlotte Brontë
Lord Jim	Joseph Conrad
Oliver Twist	Charles Dickens
The Stone Junk	Retold by D.H. Howe
Stories of Shakespeare's Plays 1	Retold by N. Kates
The Talking Tree and Other Stories	David McRobbie
The Treasure of the Sierra Madre	B. Traven
True Grit	Charles Portis

Grade 2

Vocabulary restricted to 3100 headwords
Illustrated in colour

The Adventures of Tom Sawyer	Mark Twain
Alice's Adventures Through the Looking Glass	Lewis Carroll
Around the World in Eighty Days	Jules Verne
Border Kidnap	J.M. Marks
David Copperfield	Charles Dickens
Five Tales	Oscar Wilde
Fog and Other Stories	Bill Lowe
Further Adventures of Sherlock Holmes	Sir Arthur Conan Doyle

Grade 2 (cont.)

The Hound of the Baskervilles	Sir Arthur Conan Doyle
The Missing Scientist	S.F. Stevens
The Red Badge of Courage	Stephen Crane
Robinson Crusoe	Daniel Defoe
Seven Chinese Stories	T.J. Sheridan
Stories of Shakespeare's Plays 2	Retold by Wyatt & Fullerton
A Tale of Two Cities	Charles Dickens
Tales of Crime and Detection	Retold by G.F. Wear
Two Boxes of Gold and Other Stories	Charles Dickens

Gade 3

Vocabulary restricted to 3700 headwords
Illustrated in colour

Battle of Wits at Crimson Cliff	Retold by Benjamin Chia
Dr Jekyll and Mr Hyde and Other Stories	R.L. Stevenson
From Russia, with Love	Ian Fleming
The Gifts and Other Stories	O. Henry & Others
The Good Earth	Pearl S. Buck
Journey to the Centre of the Earth	Jules Verne
Kidnapped	R.L. Stevenson
King Solomon's Mines	H. Rider Haggard
Lady Precious Stream	S.I. Hsiung
The Light of Day	Eric Ambler
Moonraker	Ian Fleming
The Moonstone	Wilkie Collins
A Night of Terror and Other Strange Tales	Guy De Maupassant
Seven Stories	H.G. Wells
Stories of Shakespeare's Plays 3	Retold by H.G. Wyatt
Tales of Mystery and Imagination	Edgar Allan Poe
20,000 Leagues Under the Sea	Jules Verne
The War of the Worlds	H.G. Wells
The Woman in White	Wilkie Collins
Wuthering Heights	Emily Brontë
You Only Live Twice	Ian Fleming

Grade 4

Vocabulary within a 5000 headwords range
Illustrated in black and white

The Diamond as Big as the Ritz and Other Stories	F. Scott Fitzgerald
Dragon Seed	Pearl S. Buck
Frankenstein	Mary Shelley
The Mayor of Casterbridge	Thomas Hardy
Pride and Prejudice	Jane Austen
The Stalled Ox and Other Stories	Saki
The Thimble and Other Stories	D.H. Lawrence